THE *PROBLEM* WITH *PROBLEMS*

"THE HUMAN EQUATION"

Or How

KNOWING THE ANSWER ISN'T ALWAYS ENOUGH

Volume I of II

MITCHELL RITTER

Preface

We face today a situation we have not known before. It is the culmination of a long process and a critical moment in the great experiment that is our Democracy. Those who claim to speak for our Founders may be familiar with the words, but they ignore the context, and therefore the meaning of those words.

The very concept on which our system of government is founded emerged from the Enlightenment, a period when many of those ideals of liberty, freedom, equality gained intellectual currency. These were not abstract concepts for they represented those very values which reflected a growing self awareness, a sense of value and an aspiration to grow and progress in ways that were never so widely embraced. Oddly, these high minded ambitions came from men, most of whom were from the moneyed classes, or had profited from the exploitation of the indigenous peoples whose lands and livelihoods they had ruthlessly expropriated.   They also embraced slavery. Indeed we are a peculiar species, capable of finding rationalizations for virtually anything we endow with a righteousness handed down to us from whatever divinity we have chosen.

Seen from a psychological perspective, our history encapsulates our contradictions, our aspirations, our often blind embrace of the current definition of progress, Recently, a significant portion of the population has come to see value in going backwards to a time which no one remembers with any accuracy, but which has become the object of a nonsensical nostalgia. Whereas human progress is expressed through the breadth and depth of our understanding of the many complexities of our world, an open-mindedness, a curiosity and a desire to grow and improve, when faced with challenges which frighten us, we are quick to revert back to a less edifying world view. And in so doing, in our rush to "conserve" what we have, we have too often failed to weigh the consequences of our choices.

This too is a reflection of the strengths and weaknesses of the human mind, the aspirations and the disappointments. The former encourage progress, the latter regress. Most people believe that we can only move in one direction, with the future pulling us irrevocably forward. Yet history is replete with contradictory examples. Sadly, yet hopefully instructively, we are living such a period

If our intelligence progresses, it is by its synthetic capabilities, its broad ranging curiosity, and its tolerance of divergent views. What happens when we reject knowledge for belief, when ignorance has supplanted any thirst for understanding? Fear seizes our emotions, we seek certainty where there can be *none, simple answers to complex problems, and divisions spring up everywhere. The distance between the present and the future shrinks, and with it any understanding of the necessity to anticipate, to plan for a future that we are creating today, the consequences of which we blind ourselves to. Instead of a multi-dimensional world, it goes flat, two dimensional, binary, and our understanding of it shrivels to a point of uselessness.*

Does all of this seem rather speculative, academic, even esoteric? After all, we have no problem invoking impersonal social forces or disease models to displace any responsibility from ourselves. The process is quite simple: look back to your past, the forces that shaped you – personal and societal – the dreams and aspirations you may have abandoned. Like a plot in a novel, you will readily see how you got from there to here. In hindsight, was it really all random? Did you not consistently make similar choices to the point of revealing an obvious pattern of behavior, if only you are willing to see it.

Now consider the future. Enlightened by this new found understanding of your own perspective, see clearly where you are now and how you got there. And look to the unwritten future. Ask yourself one simple question: are you headed where you think you are, where you would like to be, or are you following a course someone else set for you long ago? This can be a harsh realization, but only if what you feel is fear and not opportunity.

In a nutshell, that is the problem with problems. Choice. Clarity. Honesty. Authenticity.

It is true that many things escape our control. We need to know them, acknowledge them, and then set them aside, for we can't change what we don't control. What do we control? Ourselves. But to do that involves courage, conviction, and a sense of both purpose and direction in our lives without which, we abandon whatever portion of control we actually do have.

Reality is a cognitive construct based on our sensory organs and our ability to synthesize something that imposes a comprehensible structure on chaos – or our term for that part of reality which escapes us entirely. It is the only way we manage to get through our lives. That ability, however, is contingent on our perceptions, our experiences, our memories allowing us to look outside ourselves with an ever increasing clarity.

There is also an inner reality, and unconscious realm that is undeniably present, yet which the conscious mind views are useless, even threatening. After all, we don't know where it resides, why it's there, what are its imperatives and functions? Consciousness see is at elusive, contradictory, fantastical, unreliable, and obeying none of the rules of the physical world we call reality.

Yet, it is undeniably there, manifesting itself whenever we are caught off guard, when the normal filters which block our perception of it falter, or when whatever message it is sending is so close to the truth, that it cannot be ignored – these are the obvious facts which cannot, yet which continue, to e ignored.

Rejected by science, denied by research, subjugated to a symptomatology which has no, and seeks no readily available explanation, it refuses to go away. Adopted perhaps by those now considered "out there," or unscientific, too many have embraced the rejection and rode the wave out to sea.

Jung, in my opinion, came closest to having an inclusive vision of the personality, where the many apparent contradictions fit together in an interactive model. The conscious mind, having emerged with great difficulty from the "alogical" unconscious – itself a world of evocation, of metaphor, of pure creation and imagination – lives in constant fear of sinking back into what it perceives to be chaotic. Nothing renders more ignorant than fear, and the conscious mind, with all its intellectual pretensions, is not immune to its effects or consequences.

Rather, Jung saw balance where others saw pathology. The two parts – conscious and unconscious – are meant to function in a complementary manner, correcting the exaggerated perceptions of a conscious mind, ever fearful.   Yet how unnecessary this fear is, for the unconscious is the domain where we can solve any problem, imagine any solution, create something new from what never existed before. Its capacity to retain and reactivate impressions and memories is unlimited by either time or space – when left unfettered. It is the ultimate resource.   It is the repository of the very essence of our individuality. And it knows no fear, for no harm can come to it.

It has but one mission – to exist, to maintain balance, and to offer up a means of dealing with almost any situation.   A panacea? Of course not, for life is not benevolent. And not every solution is ideal. But when faced with an obstacle, and we see it as a challenge and not a problem, imbued with all the negativity the word conveys, we enter the realm of the possible.   To remain in the world of problems, to seek to eliminate or avoid them, translates readily into a declaration of regression, a rejection of progress, and a state of affairs not far off from where we are today..

I wrote much of what follows to provide some insight into how that all works on the individual level. Science may seek to deny it because it can't explain it rationally, and therefore, like the conscious/unconscious conflict, it fears what it cannot control, remaining blind to its fundamentally positive purpose. Individuals too often fear who they are "inside," being ignorant *of any other way of looking at the very different language the unconscious uses – metaphorical essentially. And society, being a rational construct, is also at odds with the unconscious because its many diverse manifestations can appear clothed in a language we don't understand. Yet when we ignore the unconscious messages, mostly by repressing them, denying them, we are refusing to listen to ourselves. And when we repress something, it doesn't go away. It lingers in the shadows, frustrated and taking on ever more primal forms, waiting for an opportunity to stage an insurgency.*

This isn't some theoretical construct. If you think back to your own past, and with an open mind, you will no doubt begin to recognize denied patterns that, because they have been denied, they continue to exercise a considerable influence on how we see reality, and therefore the choices we make.

I realize this is not a simple concept to grasp. Not because it is complicated or unnecessarily convoluted. Rather, it is because we have lost the direct access we have had in the past to our inner selves. Perhaps the form it took seemed irrational to our more quantitative, empirical, scientifically oriented current mindset. But if you imagine both working together, conscious/unconscious and mind/heart, the road to progress appears more clearly.

We have lost our way on so many levels. But in a real democracy, it belongs to each individual too know themselves as the key ingredient to know others. Democracy is collaborative, not competitive, which it has sadly become. We sink or swim together. It's time to start looking first into ourselves to better understand others to forge a more collaborative road of progress.

What follows is a series of commentaries on these questions, but from the perspective of individual responsibility and the reasons why it is happening.

From a Jungian perspective –embracing what we don't know and yet want to understand, from the bottom up, not the top down, from the evocative and not always the explicative, and from the inductive and not the reductive mind – there are new horizons, new solutions, new doors to open if only we dare. But to dare, we must find the courage to truly care.

AUTHOR'S NOTE

This is the first of two volumes entitled "THE PROBLEM WITH PROBLEMS." Is there really so much to say on the subject? Can there be any doub?. What do we love to talk about, complain about, regret, dismiss, ignore, impose, embrace, reject, let ourselves be defined by, receive from others?... ... the list is endless.

My goal here was not to address every one. That would be an impossible task. What I can do, and what I hope I will have led you to examine is how we look at problems, and why so many of us find it impossible to remedy, or at least reduce, the impact they have on our lives.

Mine is not a programmatic, symptoms based approach for I believe that is part of the problem and not the solution. Unless and until we have cleared our minds of all the clutter, distractions, falsehoods about ourselves others have put forward as quick and easy solutions, there is no way we can effectively find a clearer vision of our own stories.

Each one of us has one, a past, a present, and indeed, a future if choose to make it our own. There is a plot line which is clear to the careful observer who is rarely ourselves. To look back into our past to see how we got from there to here offers an entirely new perspective anddoor to a different future. And once that piece of the puzzle has become not only visible to, but also manageable by us – and not through a pill or a program alone –we can begin to plot a way forward to a future of our own, and not one imagined for us by others.

Mitchell Ritter

New York City , 2019

For A Very Good Friend

As I was finishing my review of this work, someone very close to me chose to leave this world. We had been friends, good friends, for close to two years. Over time he, who trusted no one, revealed to me his suffering, his pain, his solitude, for certain conditions of his life had led him to live a life that wasn't his own. To the outside world, he was fun loving, entertaining, engaged, even a of a Peter Pan. And he was good at convincing his friends and his family to the point that everyone thought that was exactly who he was.   He was successful at this in part because they wanted him to be for to see him would have meant to see themselves. But it wasn't *who* he was. It was *what* he was.

Who he was came from the demands of his family, and the compromise he found to ward off their well intentioned, yet cruelly violent, assaults. As I often told him, he was splitting himself in two, and as the gap grew wider, so too would it become harder to keep the two together. He knew all of this, knew my words were true, and protested more than promised he wanted to change.   But he couldn't.

I wrote many of these poems inspired by his experience, and though I tried in every way I knew to get him over that invisible line that separates the past from the future, he couldn't do it. There are too many like him to one degree or another.. And the price he paid, the sacrifice to those dark forces holding him back, making it impossible for him to own himself, continues to be paid by too many others.

I will miss him for he was perhaps the son I never had, and that best friend we all long to find. Though suicide is always partly a selfish act, for those who are left behind always bear some regret. And though I know there was nothing more I could have done – that is just the joint – I can't help wishing there was. He had a choice, and perhaps the time to make it had come.

I was deeply affected by this violent act his was a sweet soul that no one wanted. It was the other one, the mask, who finally claimed the place that was to have been his.

He deserved better, and dedicate this to him, his memory, and to the future he should have had.

for DARREN

T

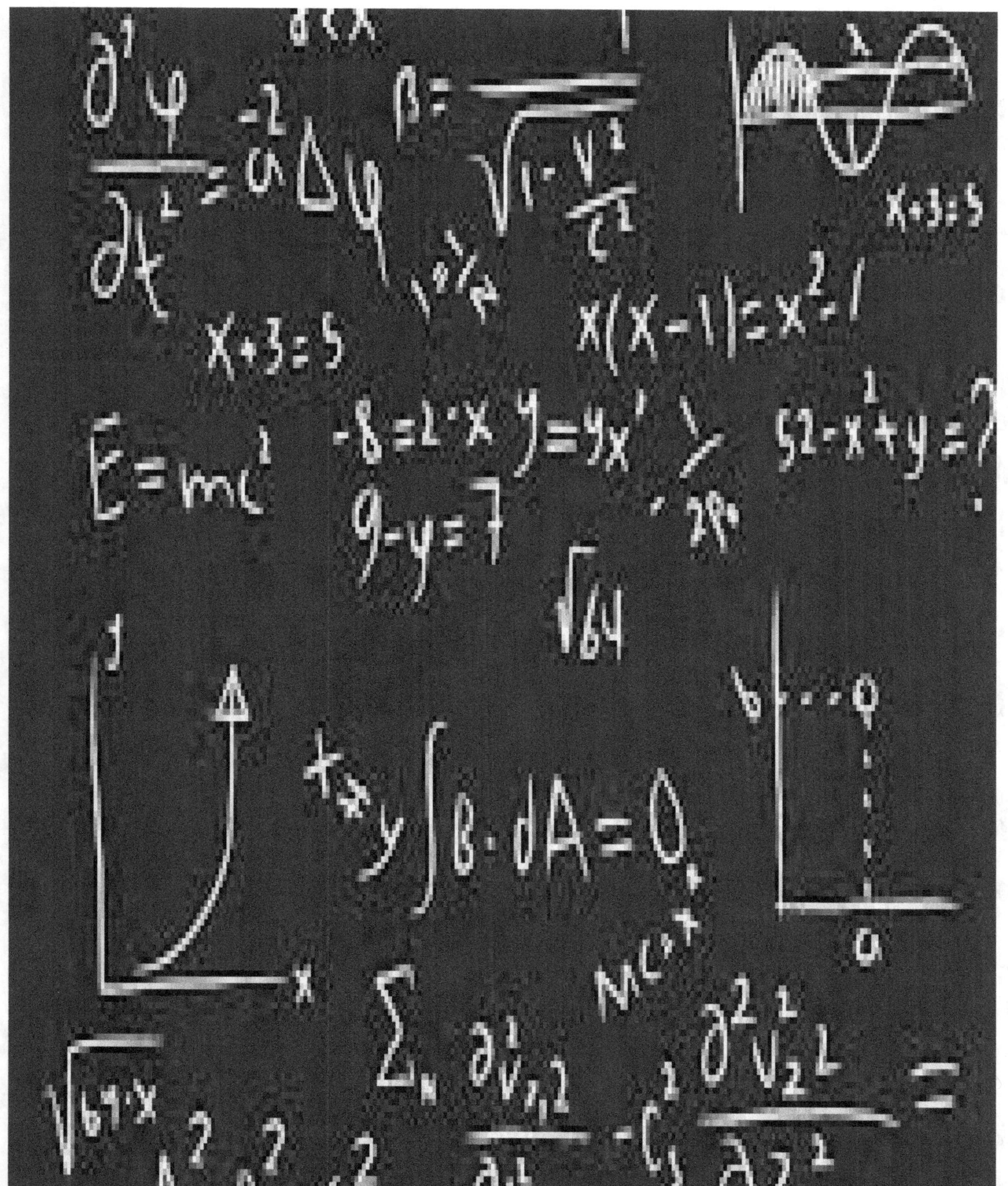

$\frac{\partial^2 \psi}{\partial t^2} = c^2 \Delta \psi$
$\beta = \sqrt{1 - \frac{v^2}{c^2}}$
X+3=5
X+3=5
X(X-1)=X^2-1
$E=mc^2$
-8=2·X y=yx' 52-x+y=?
9-y=7
$\sqrt{64}$
$\int B \cdot dA = 0$
$\sqrt{64+x}$

"Everything becomes simple after we've sorted through our own complications."

"But the problem with problems is how we view ourselves as being able to make the necessary changes"

"The past is rich with memories and experience. Some are good. Others less so. The will forms the tram on which our lives are woven."

Well intentioned adults deliver an image of ourselves which is one seen through a filter of their own. The result is we set off in life with a set of seriously false assumptions. It's only when we can jettison them that our own life begins.".

"It comes down to whether or not we find the faith in ourselves to challenge the past and dare to build a different future"

"If we don' manage to recognize who is really whispering those words of doubt in our ears, and know it is not us, how can we ever find the courage to be ourselves?"

"If you can't answer the question why you do something, then who is really holding the tillar?"

"Blood, though thicker than water, can be so much more toxic."

THE PROBLEM WITH PROBLEMS

Or

Why Being Right Isn't Enough

The end of the year is fast approaching, and I promised myself that this year I would make a change. Why? Because I'm tired of everything I do ending up the same, inconclusive way. I just needed to know why before I could uncover the what. Some friends tell me not to think about it so much. Others advise acceptance – "it is what it is." But though I have forged ahead in life in an individual and enriching manner, there is one nut I have yet to crack. It's the issue of change. Not so much for myself, for change has been a too frequent companion. But for those whose paths I've crossed in my life.

The endings always seem to be the same, regardless of what I did. The first impulse would be to blame the other person. But the real answer, without disqualifying the complexities one encounters with others who may not aspire to the same level of understanding, is that I am the constant in the equation and the only element over which I have control.

Obviously, this is by far not my interrogation alone. If anecdotal evidence based on a not insignificant sample derived from my own experience, as well as that of others, is acceptable, the fact is that we all have something about ourselves, some aspect of our lives we would like to change. And some of us even know – or think we know - what it is. The problem is that we don't seem to be able to take that extra step.This collection is a reflection on different dimensions of change, with examples of how some, and certainly not always myself, have tried. This is not a self-help book with a program, steps or answers. I believe knowledge of all kinds begins and ends with asking the question why. People who think providing answers is the way to go are, in my opinion, missing the most important part, and are depriving those who follow their counsel, of the most essential element of their journey. To use a medical metaphor, it's as if we were to stop at the symptom without any investigation of the cause. I have a very personal example to offer:

Some three years ago, I suffered a spontaneous retinal detachment. I was referred to a hospital where a surgeon performed the standard repair. Within two weeks, a spontaneous recurrence surprised everyone. A second surgery was performed – the same as the first. Three weeks later - a second recurrence. A third surgery was performed, and as before, a few weeks went by before yet another detachment happened. This went on over a period of three months. After the fifth recurrence, the ophthalmologist wanted to do the same procedure a sixth time. Suddenly I realized what was going on. She was executing the standard protocol for retinal detachments – she was treating the symptom. But she never looked into the actual cause.

I consulted another, more experienced ophthalmologist who immediately looked for the cause, identified it, and successfully repaired the detachment. Yet, even he fell into the same trap.

Focused on repairing the retina – now surgery 6 and 7 – he "forgot" to consider the entire situation, i.e. trauma to the eye, toxicity of part of his treatment to the cornea. So after the 7th surgery, when I was expecting to be finally through this 10 month ordeal, I was informed that I would now need a corneal transplant… I will spare you the rest of the saga and it's most unfortunate ending. But the point I am making is simply this: if we don't know "why", then the "what" we choose runs the serious risk of engendering, even if the obvious problem is addressed, an even greater problem.

What happened to me, and what happens when standard protocols, superficial solutions, or quick fixes are invoked, generally involving a purely quantitative approach, they tend to be formulaic, and seductive through their simplicity, they are in fact incomplete, inadequate, and little more than a band aid covering a more serious problem.

Who is at fault here? I know that is a difficult subject our culture prefers to avoid. Yet it is an essential one. In my case, I was at fault for failing to see the obvious. I was seduced by the care and attention I was given. This does not excuse the physician for her mistakes and ignorance. But if I fail to own my part, will I have learned anything from this costly experience? Of course it will always be easiesr to blame someone else, but then what am I saying about myself? It is this refusal of our role in our own lives, this delegation of choice and denial of consequence , that seems to have infected our psychology.

The problem with problems begins and ends with each of us. Life provides experiences for us to learn not to avoid or deny, and few things enrich us more than our mistakes – so long as we acknowledge ownership. Complaints about being too busy, ignorant, angry and resentful, are decoys designed to deceive. They cry out "victim." The deceit leads us to a state of dependency, denial, delegation and ultimately is not the sign of a mature and responsible population. And that is of the greatest significance for every one of us as the nation whose values we proclaim, we fail to include them in our lives any longer.

A people, a nation, that has grown so self-satisfied that it ceases to question, to pursue values of merit and not purely fortune, to care and think about the consequences of its actions, such a people has mortgaged a lesser future for a more gratifying present. It Is essential for us all to maintain a sufficient distance between the present and the future so as to be sure to understand the absolute necessity to think beyond the moment. For if one thing is clear, it is that every action brings with it a series of consequences. Some are desired. Others are not. We can live with both as long as we have acknowledged both. It Is the only reliable perception of reality, and the essential component of any good decision or choice. Without it, we will be nothing but a series of failures, disappointments, or worse.

Good luck to us all in the hope that we find our way home, and soon.

CONTENTS

INTRODUCTION

The Problem with Problems is both a complex and a simple one, depending on where one starts. Fundamentally, problems are a part of life, and how we deal with them goes a long way in defining the kind of life we have and how satisfied we are with it. In essence, it is a matter of attitude and perception.

That being said, problems are real things, some of which we control directly, others arrive on their own. But there is a third kind, and they will be the principal focus of this collection. What does that mean? In every circumstance, there is a choice, no matter how large or small. And these choices will invariably have an impact on the outcome. The question is what forces, unconscious for the vast majority, will blind us to their existence or allow us to see them. And in a second moment, even if we do see them, whether we will find the resources to act constructively on them. This is the key to the subtitle of this work, i.e. being right isn't always enough.

Change is a constant in most people's conversation. Everyone has something about themselves or their lives they'd like to change. We can't change the past, so many people just assume, as the saying goes "..it is what it is."   It is indeed true insofar as the facts are concerned. But what is not true, indeed is so terribly false, is that there is nothing we can do about how we understand past events. Seeing how their influence continues to direct our choices, the degree to which we have so embraced them as to have become blind to our own potentialities remain driving forces in our lives. Recognize them, and we will have gained an added measure of choice in our lives.

These composite decisions, or compromises, represent the best possible solution to a given problem at a moment in time   Best possible is not ideal. It means simply that we managed to obtain the most of what we wanted, what we needed as an expression of ourselves. Compromises, however , can often be flawed when we are forced to give up too much of our essential selves to satisfy the demands of othrs. More sublte, however, are those compromises formed when we were children, becoming perceptions of ourselves, when our means of imposing our will was limited. Normally, as we grow in strength and knowledge, they are naturally amended to reflect a growing independence and need of r self-realization.

Now there is a term one doesn't hear much anymore, and It still sounds "New Agey", even to me. What I mean when I use it is to acknowledge that each of us is not so and so's son or daughter, or have a parent's personality. That is simply impossible for we are a blend of two halves, and the likelihood that both halves being identical is null.   What happens is that parents project   - unconsciously – their own unfulfilled dreams and aspirations onto their children, and thinking that in so doing, they will both repair their own disappointments, and sure for their offspring the future the parents wished they had had.

The constant pressure exercised on children is necessary for their own development and we must not forget that they also have the ability to assert their own desires by means any parent will be happy to explain. The problem intervenes when the parental pressure is too great, ultimately defeating, crushing, enslaving a child by robbing it of any kernel of confidence in its own ability to prevail anywhere. When this happens, one of two things can happen. Either the child so fully embraces the parental image that it becomes a clone. But this "compromise" promises serious problems down the road for we all need to retain some connection to that unique blend of genetic material and external influence that makes each one of us one of a kind. Cutting that connection through this identification - which is the same thing as a renunciation of oneself – deprives any person of the foundation necessary for anything but a superficial identity. In other words, we will have created a shell, but one with no substance, no fire, no desire.

The other option is total rebellion where something in the child remains preserved from th parental pressures, and will seize on any means to oppose – even to the point of self-destruction - any parental directive – even the most appropriate and beneficial. In this way, a child is also deprived of a constructive connection to their essential selves, for though they will have retained some strength, they will have nothing positive to direct it towards. A dark picture indeed. And, of course, there is the full spectrum (today's popular term) in between.

It is in this field of battle that exists, in some degree for all of us, that will be found the *problem with problems*. How it expresses itself, how it is address, how it is resolved – or not – will determine the outcome of every life. Yet we seem blissfully unaware of what is going on, choosing most often to actually direct our attention away from it. There are many personal, cultural and gender issues which influence those decisions.   But one thing is certain.   The consequences can be dire. We have adopted, the role they continue to play, and just how much they cost us. In a few words, it's a question of whether we have delegated our future to the past, relegated ourselves to some "other" version of ourselves that can only be inherently in conflict with who we would otherwise have become, and acquiesce in the perpetuity of a bad situation.

One can adopt different perspectives on the same central issue. I often focus on power: just how powerless or powerful we may feel. And often, wounds of the past have an unfortunate effect on that very sentiment.   Starting in childhood, an acute state of powerlessness, yet a self-centeredness creates a situation in flux where boundaries are defined. It is not simply a matter of clarity, but also of degree.

A child growing up in a family where there are few boundaries, a sense of self-importance will emerge. But being only a child with little understanding of how the larger world works, not to mention that if parents don't carry that load, a child will have to. In this situation, we have a top heavy, over-confident child who does not have the solid foundation parents must provide. The stereotypical Millenial is a good example.

On the other hand, we may have a parental presence that is so dominant, so overbearing, so imposing that the child has no chance to preserve its integrity, but must comply with every requirement encountered, no matter how arbitrary of extreme. With no recourse, no sense of their own power or importance develops, leaving he child with a vision of themselves as perennial victims, even slaves, to whatever master is present. Since there can be no direct opposition, and total submission is rare, the child will develop a passive form of resistance which will lead them to never be up to the standards required by the parent. In essence, this means an already oppressed child will further amputate itself in terms of its potential and ambition. It is a negative self-affirmation, itself at odds with the child's original and innate sense of itself. In describing the two extremes, the range of possibilities existing between the two is quite large. That being said, the number ofr people having experienced these extremes far greater than we might care to believe.

So what might this middle ground look like? Compliance would be operative principal. Compromise might be another good adjective to describe the phenomenon. We affect such arrangements when presented with a situation we don't want to accept yet know we cannot refuse completely. Compromise can, of course, be an expression of a good relationship to reality, as long as it doesn't cost too much. If it does, we have entered a dangerous territory where conflict between our inner selves and our outside lives is manifest.

Being forced to turn against ourselves to satisfy external demands is equivalent to doing ourselves violence. And the result is either a successful assimilation at the time, or a profound resentment. The anger felt can either be absorbed, directed against the external source, or against oneself in the form of a self-destructive type of guilt. If successful and not too costly, the experience can promote a solid perception and a healthy, balanced relationship with reality. In this case, things should progress smoothly. If not, too much of oneself is sacrificed, forced back into the unconscious where it will seethe and fester until it overwhelms the mask the person will have been forced to wear. It prevents sincerity, authenticity, trust and intimacy.

Incapable of these key elements of human existence, a future less than fulfilling, if not frankly unhealthy, awaits. For the individual will not be equipped to constructively respond to life's challenges, wherein the Problem with Problems.

Of course we need to learn to control ourselves, to channel our energies in ways other than our primal urges might suggest. Compromise is a middle ground, a viable course, and one that allows us to live and even to some degree, to thrive in society. This requires that we not come to identify with our problems, we don't let them define us in terms of the self-image we develop throughout or lives.

This self-image is often an unconscious "sanity check" we perform when confronted with any given situation. It is also the model we attempt to emulate because having seen someone else behave in a certain way and find success in so doing, it is perfectly normal to want to follow a similar path to a similar outcome. To admire is to want to emulate. And if that is not possible, to find some indirect way to participate (this being a teaser for a future discussion of the infamous "chemistry" many consider to be the mysterious and unknowable explanation for attraction).

But there is a problem here too, for if we look outward for answers, we tend to distance ourselves from that essential part of ourselves which is there in a rudimentary form, but present nonetheless. If, during the course of our lives we sanction our own impulses without understanding them, and model ourselves only on what we see outside ourselves, we quite simply lose touch with who we are.

Is this really that important? Life demands a certain constant, a center, a sense of some core and a minimum of coherence of being as we transition through life's phases. If at each juncture we modify ourselves in the hope of attaining whatever we think we want without some consistency and continuity, then a new question become entirely relevant. Who are we? And if we don't know who we are, how can we possibly know what we, ourselves, need and want? And so we double down against this intolerable confusion and indecision through an avidiity, a versatiity, and a lack of clarity that will render us lost in our own lives.

Today, we use material acquisitiveness as the means to contain this sense of loss and loneliness. The quantitative, in all its forms has replaced the more qualitative vision. More is the answer, rather than why or why. The problem is that the solution is maladapted. If one is alienated from oneself, buying more expensive, more exclusive care will not provide any solid and durable sense of self. Continuing to search for it there is a fool's errand because it is never-ending as avidity is related to envy, and envy is fed by a competitive outlook with any true sense other than to acquire, to collect. The flow of new, better or more exclusive is itself never ending. Those who follow this path are chasing their own tails, and will exhaust themselves in the process while making only negative progress, i.e. regression, against what they really need.

Does a true self exist? Not in some absolute, fully formed manner. But that a set of essentials come into the world with us and are there to define us, seems undeniable. The notion of a child being a tabula rose – a blank slate – has been abandoned long ago. The undeniable fact of our inter-individual diversity, no matter how numerous we are, should be proof enough. There is unquestionably a "me" in there somewhere. Finding it, understanding it, discovering opportunities for it to express itself in the real world, remaining always in touch with it, these are the expressions of what we used to consider as destiny, karma or fate. We used to project them onto the external world in the form of Gods, or other metaphysical entities. Though useful to refer to them metaphorically, we can be certain of only one thing. Our lives must become our own, though we live together in a chaotic world. We were given the means to survive and even prosper. The challenge is to use those means and not seek to deny them. To do so makes us less than we are, could be, indeed need to be.

We have gone a long way down the wrong path. What species can survive if it fails to embrace itself, to evolve from our origins to something higher. To go in the opposite direction promises only one thing. That the world will start to resemble once again what it was in the past when it was a far more dangerous place than today.

Whether a professional or simply an individual curious about the issue of change, beware the easy answer. They are everywhere and easy to find. But the will to change, the motivation, the means one is ready to deploy, the sacrifices and uncertain one will encounter in building a new reality for real, these are the things that will determine whether or not change will happen.

This is an inspirational, a hopeful, possibly even a heroic way of looking at life. Philosophers have examined this issue over the ages and have come up with a broad range of answers. But that's just the point. An answer points only the way. It is only in mobilizing the necessary resources that one's perception of the world and how it works, one's place in it, and how susceptible to having an impact can be altered. It is only in doing that old experiences are replaced with ew ones, the only means of reestablishing a healthier sense of reality.

A therapist's work lies not in unlocking the mystery of one's behavior. That's relatively easy. They can provide support, confidence, hope and conviction. But unless the person is ready to let go of the past and look to a new future without the boundaries that were protective walls in -the past, having over time become prison walls, little of any real meaning can happen. That is the promise and the disappointment of therapy. There is no cure. There is only living as knowingly, as constructively and as positively as we can.

THE PROBLEM WITH PROBLEMS

November 2018

These most recent writings, like most of the poems themselves, coalesced around a theme which essentially imposed itself on me. I write to think, to find answers to the questions of human behavior which I and everyone encounters every day. The difference is that, for reasons of training and predilection, I seek and find patterns that most others simply don't notice. My previous writings dealt with a range of different issues, but somehow this brings me back to my very first short story – -"Mr. Hide's Progress." It's a story about why people make bad choices. The answer I came up with, based on a failed relationship I watched unfold, was fear on the one part, and a certain overconfidence bordering on the innocent on the other. They represented two poles, two extremes of the same thing: light and darkness.

And at the time, that seemed to have put the question to rest. In the time since that writing, what was superficially obvious, became more profoundly so, as the "pathology of everyday life," a famous book written by Freud also noticed (more insightful for its title than its content). However, there are a few fundamental differences.

First, to approach things as pathological is to miss the fact that in so doing, one neglects that pathology is a process and not a static state. Insofar as one entered it from a "normal" beginning, it is conceivable that one could find a way back. Though this is obviously an ideal, it is nonetheless true that even if a "cure," another static state, most likely will not be achieved – for journeys leave scars that alter us all –

personality is not a bone or a diseased organ that is physically destroyed.

Our minds are plastic, malleable, and the most adaptive organ (in its function, less so in its embodiment) we possess. Seeing how someone came to be in a state of psychological distress and dysfunction, and I'm not referring to neurochemistry here but one's life story, can chart a way back. That way back is not to the initial state – reversibility exists in logic, not in biology – but back towards a more coherent sense of self. Without this coherence, one cannot produce the consistency reality requires.

Second, and this is a message to anyone seeking to help, posing a diagnosis can be a therapeutic, observational act, or it can be a statement of personal inadequacy. The very essence of our personalities requires that we be in some form of connection with another of our kind. Diagnosing someone based on protocols is the ultimate act of disconnection. It will alter how one listens, how one reacts, what one can learn about oneself and the other. Though it may sound authoritative, it is building a wall between the two individuals who need most to connect.

And third, I find that our society has embarked on a journey into darkness, a pseudo-scientific reductionism based on essentially a quantitative analysis when what is needed is a more qualitative approach. Why? Because what is quantitative seeks normalization, a leveling so as to establish categories one can then populate with groups of individuals – the key being groups. For it is the group then that is described and not the individual. That part is sacrificed for an average that may exist statistically, but who probably doesn't even exist

There may be excesses when indulging in the qualitative, for it is by definition an assembly of unrelated variables which will not be willingly forced into arbitrary categories. One can easily get lost in the weeds. But that is why we have a mind – to understand without blindly embracing, to discern from careful observation of oneself and the othe,r subtleties which reveal the essential keys, and to synthesize from these seemingly disparate elements a coherent whole. It is inductive, not deductive, leaving open the door to, however much we think we know, all that remains to be discovered.

So what's not working? In trying to approach things differently, being more observational, more qualitative, I meet by chance the person I dedicated this work to. It was through his struggles, his ambivalence, his deft us of deflection and distraction, the unholy compromise he had established early on that worked then, but which as is often the case, fails to evolve with the individual was revealed. This deal with the devil became ossified, a bone instead of a muscle, a structural part of his personality which preferred to break rather than bend.

How did this happen? He simply used his problems to define a position, a compromise with his environment, that allowed him to disrupt its demands and efforts while allowing him some space to assert himself. It was by no means an healthy situation, but he could survive. But compromises like this are not flexible – they are fixed, static, and rigid. People are meant to be the opposite. So as he grew, the compromise did not. And it stunted him in ways he only began to suspect until it was almost too late. For being structural, it defined him, and he identified with it. Or at least part of him did.

To intervene, to risk the bone had become impossible because an essential part of the compromise was never to try and change it. He never learned to test his strength, his ability to be free, and found himself weak – his own terms. And from this self-image, this place of ancient safety, now a prison, there was no reserve of strength he could call upon, and no infusion of strength from someone else could save him.

When we identify with our problems, when our self-image is so linked to them, that actually doing something concrete to change them represents a threat to one's own identity, we are facing a high wall indeed.. The conundrum creates an impossible situation whereby maintaining the problem comes to be recognized as oneself. The war is lost before it began. The problem with problems. Perverse indeed.

I've always believed we meet the people we need to meet. I had no plan to follow this path until it became an imperative through this friendship. It took two years for it to come together. But it came at a high price. I hope others can benefit from what was a tragic journey, an unhappy life, and a wasted future. He was not alone. We all have problems – it's part of life. But some of us are given a chance. And others are not.

We say there is always hope, and indeed that is true. But within the "always," there are moments more propitious than others. Time, however, is not infinite, and always has an end as much as it has a beginning. Such is also true of a nation. One should always be mindful not to wait until it is too late.

There are days when our lives seems made of these

Rarely alone, quietly, they arrive like an infectious disease

They appear at moments often inopportune

Following a variable cycle not unlike that of the moon

They have no specific shape common to their kind

And sneak up on our side that's blind

They can come from friend or foe alike

Without much warning they can strike

Some more imagined than concrete and real

But the fear of them we always feel

Wishing they would go away

Yet they persevere and too often stay

Some may, on their own, disappear

"Wait them out" is advice we sometimes hear

But whether they return or refuse to leave

The more complex and layered persist and deceive

A truth they bear, though we seek to deny

Their refusal to be gone our efforts belie

Ironic how their origin we disguise with our lie

Hoping somehow on this accommodation to rely

Often mistaken for a riddle with no solution

Though try as we may, we find no resolution

The most resistant can lead us ultimately

To a wall or a door beyond which we cannot see

Some struggle their whole life long

Imagining an improved version of themselves, so to belong

The truth is there, staring them in the face

Yet blind they remain, of the road ahead they find no trace

Passive and stuck, for some answer they wait

Hope abdicated, their lives set by Fate

Time advances and it's getting late

Compromise directs them to a different gate

Though it may seem an easier way

"Who needs to prove one's worth?" or so they say

Forgetting it is only what is earned is truly owned

Which would you prefer? The original or the cloned?

Reprieves may come from time to time

An opportunity to reflect perhaps and mine

All that came before that brought them here

And find a way the confusion to clear

When things are good, and the skies look blue

Why worry when things are fine and problems few?

It's better now, why look back?

Now that everything is once again on track

Problem solved, why return to some forgotten past?

I've turned the page, these problems were not meant to last

Ignore them and watch now how the dye is cast

Problems deferred, overlooked or simply outcast

Can they really ever disappear?

Or do they lie in wait, in the shadows near?

Waiting for a time that's opportune

To strike again and burst the balloon

A choice by default is still a choice, one we can't ignore

The answer is often there, behind that door

We have the key, but fear to look

Habits form quickly, and that's all it took

Without some terrible fear to motivate

Unaware of just how in the game it's late

This too we've learned to not see

Has any form of blindness ever set us free?

What is it that scares us so?

That we renounce a chance to know

Are we afraid of some future waiting at the end of the road?

Is the present more attractive as it seems to offer a lighter load?

Is that the reason the future recedes?

And we focus so much on present needs

Tomorrow comes, no one can avoid

The unknown waits and is never destroyed

The thing we want most not to see

Waiting there it will surely be

But as long as I can pretend

This recess I call my life I hope will never end

Part II

So after a rest from the latest reversal

Believing that Life is just a rehearsal

Actors in our own lives of make believe

We grow more shallow, as if to relieve

Yet when clouds form and uncertain winds rise

Where to find the answers and surmise

From whence does strength truly come?

Is it true of late we prefer to run?

The more fear we have to take a look

As if written in some mysterious book

Recalling at the very thought the foundations shook

As we slink away in fear, our strength as well it took

Though the scene be repeated time and again

The future may wait – but until when?

Sooner or later reality will bite

It can come in the day. More likely in the dead of night

The stars align forcing open your eyes

Will fools they forever be or see the need to be wise?

Can it be these souls in themselves are less invested?

Having no taste for life's true challenges and to remain tested?

To know at last of what they are made

Will they rise and shine, or retreat and fade?

Will they lower their sails and the anchor drop?

Will this be the moment when their lives come to a stop?

Others, for reasons for you to explore

Fill their souls with a hunger to learn more

For some to emulate others might be enough

For them they've had their fill of fluff

Substance alone can keep them fed

They push onward with anticipation, not dread

Some imagine life offers a guarantee

Success is assured and with a warranty

Life's challenges are only opportunities

It's only in living for real one learns and sees

But what of those raised in the sun?

They've no need to struggle, nor want to run

Or of those who know only reversal and defeat

Who lack the essentials but still tried to stand on their own feet

Who was right, who was wrong

I've got the music, but not the lyrics to the song

That, my friend, must be yours alone to write

My words offer perspective, not some simple answer "lite"

Consumers are we and we get to choose

Risk alone defines if we win or lose

To win is to have done one's best

To have run the good race and met the test

We assume the result requires we finish first

It's for that alone that we thirst

Will losing cause the bubble to burst?

Not to have run at all, that's the worst

To run requires we know our strengths

And our weaknesses, to help us extend the lengths

To go as far as we possibly can

Is that not a working definition of what it is to be a man?

A vision heroic perhaps, I am not so sure

An idealization of a life worthy and a legacy that can endure

Once again, faced we are with a choice

To be spoken out loud, and with a strong voice

In terms that endure and cannot be spent

Not on food or clothing or even the rent

How we respond defines the currency of the soul

Whether we finish in debt, or if our lives have made us whole

MARRIAGE/DIVORCE/CHILDREN

September 2018

This poem began with an idea around the old Greek myth of Athena springing full grown from her father, Zeus' brow. It is the story of a father's fantasy about the perfect woman: a daughter, wise, pure, with nothing sexual about her. This relieves the father of any confusion regarding his child's gender, her maturing into adulthood, and her eventual passage to another man. An odd story indeed. It is also the story of a father's desire to rob his wife of her essential role in procreation. As King of the Gods, he wanted to be truly all powerful. A male fantasy if ever there was one.

There were elements which were common to my experience as a father insofar as though my ex-wife executed her responsibilities, there was more female rivalry (in her mind towards her daughters) than maternal love. At best, it was ambivalent. At its worst, it was an outright competition.

Being the only man in the family, affinities intervened and shifted as the children grew up, and as my role expanded to ensure not only the traditional providing, guiding, supporting, protecting, to something more akin to what Zeus sought. I had a very different vision of women than is common in Switzerland, partly due to my family background, my culture, and my own somewhat idealized vision of women. In short, insofar as their mother represented a certain embrace of dependence, powerlessness, an identity based on victimhood and the renunciation of her own capabilities, I tried to give my daughters a sense that they could do whatever they set their minds to.

Over time, the contradiction between parents crystallized into a father living his own version of his ambition, his confidence in himself, and the sense of capacity and a mother whose "power" derived from her displaying just the opposite – her weakness, her lack of confidence, her incompleteness, and of course the manipulative way in which she played on these elements.

As with most men, these dispositions were evident to my mother, but not to men. The power of seduction, the propensity of men to see their masculinity validated when called upon by a woman for help, and the indirect nature of male/female communication, all were in evidence and not to be underestimated.

The question in this poem was the concern I had for my daughters and how they had assimilated my relationship with their mother as a role model for their own adult relationships, how the manipulations of their mother affected their own self-images, and how their mother's ambivalence towards being a woman with two daughters would influence their own maternity. A father can see just so much, and therefore can do just so much.

What I can, and have done, is to insist on something which has been ignored by fathers and their children. If one truly embraces the role of father in its positive sense, then the power seen in their father can be transferred to the daughters, without passing through their mother.

Part of this transfer is a legitimate "debt of gratitude,' and acknowledgement of what was considered carefully, curated every day, and given as a sacred duty and honor to one's children. It was given without strings, per se, but nonetheless demands that it be recognized for the benefit of parent and child. If not, the parent will question himself and his child, and the child will take for granted something very precious and necessary, not only for their own lives, but for the lives of their own future children.

Too much is taken for granted in the parent/child relationship these days where parents reject the depth of their role, preferring the notion of being loved as a friend.   The eschewing of any coherent expression of parental authority plays a fundamental role in much that doesn't work in our society. One has many friends throughout one's life, but only one Father. His role is to provide and protect, to endow his children with a sense of worthiness, of their having a place reserved perhaps, but which must be earned. That which is given too freely will not be recognized, and therefore its value diminishes.

A child who has had a father who plays ball with his son when the child's mother reminds him to do so will create a doubt in the mind of the child which can constitute a significant obstacle the child may never overcome – even as an adult. Children derive their initial sense of self-worth from the attention their parents sincerely and authentically pay them. It is the foundation on which everything else will reside.

This is significant for boys, as the father is the one who show his son the way to his own manhood in its deepest sense – by the values he has chosen to live by, by his fairness, his integrity, his sense of honor, and his growing maturity which being a father will promote. These themes are omnipresent in myths where for a boy to become a man, in his head, his heard and his body, there is a preparation, then a journey of discovery, a confrontation with some incarnation of evil (generally, but not exclusively, female in nature), and an ultimate victory. But, as I have pointed out, it is significant for girls as well, for in a male dominated society, a girl needs to feel empowered by her father to believe in herself and her abilities, her value, as a woman.

As an aside, this in no way reduces the importance of a mother. But too often, we tend to gloss over a man's role in his family. If seen principally as provider, someone whose focus is work, disengaged from the development of his children, as we see in many representations of fathers in popular culture, then that is what he will become. If, however, he sees being a father himself as a means of validating his own value in society, everyone will benefit.

There is an archetypal role for the Father as the source of structure, order, power and authority. It is, of course, stereotypical, but that is the point. In our basic concept over the ages, there is both a father and a mother. Without one – in any form – there is chaos. As our experience of and as men evolves from the very clear and rigid roles we were called upon to fulfill, to a rather deconstructed vision of what it means to be a man, where options abound, the reliability of the archetype grows more vague. Some may see only the benefits of an expanding vision of what it means to be a man. But it is equally necessary to be mindful of what the cost of this period of transition may bring about.

It is a biological and psychological fact that our species exists as two genders, as defined by Nature. It exists as well in most other species, though it can vary. But this variance is supported by the physical attributes. These too cannot be ignored. If we change the roles, we change the rules, and with it, we change society as well. Something to think about as we continue on this path of deconstruction

If this seems exaggeratedly complicated, it is only insofar as I want to convey what goes on mostly on an unconscious level, but exists nevertheless. To ignore it would be derelict, for in every marriage there are so many things happening which will exercise a determining influence on their children's choice of spouse, career, character, predispositions and their own behavior with their own children. And insofar as these children become adults and active participants in some future society, what they experience will determine the course of society. Since we so often prefer to skip over what seems complicated, believing that it is either unnecessary or it will fix itself, would it not be wise to pause and consider the consequences of our actions before? .

A family is indeed a mystery

Held together by a myth of unity

When children are young

Only one song is sung

The music seems to write itself

Emerging whole, as if off the shelf

Are the notes reflective of experience past?

Believing through the years it was meant to last

Surprises await, though forewarned

So easily fooled when young, with life's illusions adorned

Time takes most of them away

Always curious which ones get to stay

Of those that remain, which ones will last?

And the characters in the plot are so often miscast

Not that they can't play their part

It's just their stories had a different start

Ignorant, we believe love is all we need

Two young lovers devoid of greed

Until such time as the glow goes pale

Watch which pieces first go up for sale

First sadness enters where once there was joy

Second, sex is no longer their favored toy

If indeed it ever was so

Who will admit it? –Will we ever know?

Some things we accept to see

The others we replace with fantasy

Thus altering the collective reality

To leave or stay or just let it be

Even then we need to shield our eyes

Whether or not clouds fill the skies

Illusions give us all direction

Replacing dreams with unnamed predilection

What once seem destined to transform

Two people into one as per the norm

Perhaps in days gone by, when choices were few

We could not distinguish what we ignored from what we knew

The ground has shifted now, so much has changed

So few things are stable, so many deranged

A union built on a lie, told by a needy spouse

All she wanted was a place to live, a home, a house

With so little in her heart, what could she ever claim?

Things would be much easier if she could wear his name

Afraid to build a life of her own was her game

What she wanted was to ride the wave of whatever was to be
his fame

And so began a web of lies

Seven years later and so many tries

She let it slip one ordinary day

"I never understood all those things you say"

Too late, the truth had escaped

It was her spouse's trust that had been raped

Naïve to the point of neglect

It never occurred there might be a lie to detect

Quickly the mask was repaired

Long conversations, as if she cared

Every chance to look inside

She'd blame her spouse and continue to hide

Hard to say how many faces she could wear

She has this strange regard that said I'll never dare

An innocent – though not innocent – the truth be told

He wanted something real before he was old

A sort of truce settled in

Only on occasion was it ever mentioned, the sin

Children grew and went with friends

Parents never know what they do and towards what ends

Then off to school and out of the nest

Then it hits, those years gone by would be the best

For once they leave, or once it was so

Their future is what they want to know

Unsuspecting, they waste no time

Full speed ahead, their lives are fine

The emotional baggage is packed and sent

Never to return home for good, how lives are bent

Left alone two strangers now

One strayed but here's why and how

Business travel made things so neat

No dalliances near home so not to defeat

That which he had fought for 20 plus years

Was to be preserved in spite of his fears

That things would never ever change

A settled life seek not to derange

But she did see it otherwise

In secret, as always, no end to the lies

I know he tried, of her I don't know

She probably had no answer, and if she did, she would not let it show

A game plan hatched with her father fear

Who she'd hated for so many a year

Resentful he took pleasure in others pain

Mean for sure, but not insane

Just another man who'd been skinned alive

Growing up in his sister's shadow, with her there he could not thrive

Once settled, the unpleasantness past

Time to build a new life for real, at last

But he'd been changed, his senses acute

Never again to give in the any needy female's flute

What of the children, what would they say?

What did they understand and take away?

At the threshold of their lives, their own

Had their hopes been stunted by the years or had they grown?

It's been many years since I returned

It took me so long to accept how I'd been burned

I've watched my children separate too

They've taken reasonable positions, as if they knew

Though I'd always spoken openly

There were things they did not care to see

So Swiss, they sought to live in neutrality

Believing from their past they could be free

One daughter more committed to me

One daughter caught in her mother's game, not free

Neither seems to care to know

That wounds require we take a stand if we are to grow

It's been a painful time, wronged I've often felt

But I am not one to freeze my feelings, I'd rather have them melt

Adults now are they, married with children of their own

A side of life to discover from the other side unknown

They have their lives, I'm now an accessory

There is one advantage now, I am free

Fatherhood never weighed me down

It made me a man – with cap and gown

I watch over them as best I can

And in the most honest of ways, I am their fan

But if wronged I am through neglect

If a lack of caring I detect

No words are spared for I have always believed

If one was truly loved and protected, from caring one cannot be relieved

Life is indeed a tale of considerable complexity

We juggle conflicting imperatives with as much dexterity

Always watching that we don't lose our way

To question and learn what we can of life every single day

No real promises are made, they were only illusions

Too young to understand, so full of our own delusions

Behind the scenes, a light burns never to be extinguished

As long as it shines on our path and points us in directions distinguished

Somehow we will find the strength and continue to believe

There is much loss in life, but not enough time to always grieve

Those who've gone have left a mark on our souls

First with joy, then with pain, no prize comes without tolls

Having known them for the time we had

How can we not be sad?

Is there more goodness for real in life?

Or more sadness and strife?

A person I once admired

Spoke not long after she retired

Asked if her success had given her the happiness we all desire

She responded knowingly, for had felt disappointment's fire

'Life is too hard for happiness to endure

I'm cheerful and with that I am satisfied and very sure"

So if this poem has left you wondering is he depressed?

My answer echoes the same thought – whether happy or distressed

it comes down to how free we feel when faced with an opposing force

Do we accept to engage and believe in married ife, and not in divorce.?

There it is, yet another choice

Has this tale made you sad or rejoice

I think therein lies the only answer

A wallflower to be or a dancer

NO LONGER LOST

September. 2018

I have a friend who I've come to know well these past 18 months, and much of what I saw him struggle with informs many of the poems – and perhaps most of all, this one. The second son of a local family, he grew up in the shadow of a rather terrifying mother. She was well motivated, had been through much growing up herself, and was determined to see to it that he children would lead lives better than her own. A noble goal indeed, though the means she deployed, according to this friend, were terrible in the true sense of the word.

The father was a man of few words whose past was only sketched out. He was an immigrant but was accepted by his wife's family for reasons principally of religion. He too felt the lash of his wife's unaccomplished ambition, to the point that this family of three men and one women lived in fear of this dragon who, if she did not breath actual fire, her words burned deep and hot nonetheless.

A mature man now, though still living as a student, he was never given the chance as a child to discover anything of himself that was not seen through his mother's eyes. He complied until a few years ago, but made sure to never measure up to his mothers requirements. His rebellion was secretive, self-destructive, contradictory, even to his own self-interest. Left with a self-image so contorted between his desire to resist his mother's demands and his own ever weakening dreams of a life of his own, I feared for his future. He now finds himself split essentially in two. One, closest to himself, is kind, hungry for affirmation and recognition, yet afraid to exercise the full extent of his abilities as a true sign of rebellion. The other is cold, angry, selfish and equally rebellious, though in ways that can prove to be self defeating if not self-destructive. As he has said himself in moments of number one's lucidity, "…I just can't get out of my own way."

Somewhat reminiscent of a previous friend about whom I wrote in "The Leftovers of God's Anger," there were two opposing forces battling for control of the young man in question. I see seeds of the same dissociative behavior, though not as serious as with Chris, for he

at a turning point in his life which will determine its future course. That being said, and though his circumstances were more obviously difficult, his hunger to survive, if for no other reason than revenge, was manifest.

If only he could find the strength to banish his number two, embrace his number one, and let go of this infernal conflict he has with his parents, this man would have a future. But he seems to evolve in cycles, not making much progress. My perspective is not of sufficient length to answer that question. But as a friend, I fight with him, or him. His is an eternal struggle in a man's search for his own masculine identity – to fee himself from the bonds of childhood. I don't know if he will be able to find his courage and face down the dragon, or if he has already succumbed. But if the myths are any indication, it is only with the assistance of a true friend, an ally, a guide who can reveal how to defeat the monster. One can give him a magical sword, a special shield, but the essential element must come from him – his belief, his courage, and his conviction that his is a worthy cause. Absent that, there will be neither victory nor freedom. Her hold on him is strong, and every time he dares to advance, she manages to douse him, not with flames, but with doubt. And that has been, at least until now, as far as he has gotten.

And what of the father? He would be the natural ally. Or even the older brother. Neither have stepped forward to help. Quite possibly they are not unhappy that my friend has been claimed as the sacrificial victim, the one even the mother said she would make her daughter. All of this he revealed to me over time. But from his friends. They had shared in the conspiracy to keep him a prisoner of the warm, funny man who loves his family. Either they are blind to his truth, or they see it and find it convenient for everyone but him. I fear he has given up on ever growing up.

To have the courage to see and to feel

To know what's true and makes things real

Though painful at first, it alone can heal

Therein lies the essential deal

Lives are built on messages sent and received

Some are sincere, spoken to be believed

Though this be true, sincerity can mislead

Depending on the agenda, the purpose and the need

Stone by stone, the edifice is built

Sometimes with love, at others with guilt

It takes years to collect and assemble the pieces

Some are enslaved, others freed only when their master releases

From the parental power will come an image imposed

Of which one's parts will be kept, others disposed

When the glue has dried and the pieces are set

We are told to be thankful and assume the debt

For who knows better who we were meant to be?

Than those who believe they own us for eternity

Whose image of us we embrace, on this they rely

No matter the cost, expected we are to comply

No longer the original me, but an adjusted version

Our true path now transformed into a diversion

Based on an image of oneself that others have made

Some parts one might need now exclude, forever forbade

We live with this image of who we are

Constantly measuring ourselves to see how far

We've strayed or approached this goal they have set

Without truly questioning if it can ever be met

For those who seeded our lives with dreams of their own

Their unfulfilled fantasies having now overgrown

Their gardens untended, things left without care

How is it that now it's left up to each one to dare?

Each of us is given gifts to achieve one goal

Specific yet requiring we somehow be whole

But if some things are taken and by others imposed

While in so doing our own dreams are deposed

A piece of ourselves is taken, though we may not know

How the confusion began, and the resistances grow

We see no clear path that points towards success

Try though we may, progress stalls, and begins to regress

Clouded are our minds, they see not clear

If we delve too deeply, we meet a familiar fear

Told we are not to waste our time

Leave it alone and things will be fine

Words such as these turn us away

From what the disorder is trying to say

Since when is it wise not to reflect?

How else can one hope to see the defect?

One where we went along, that's factually true

But the reasons why we never knew

Therein lies the fault, the choice we made

To be able to think one must see what left and what stayed

To enter the place we were told not to go

To look into not just our acts, but our motives to know

Not those that any fool can see

But those that were misunderstood though they belonged to
be me

That when it's time to ask how we arrived in this place

Does it reflect the image I see when I gaze in my face?

How much of a lie have we all become?

You'll know the answer if the answer is none

To try to be someone other than we were meant to be

Is a mission impossible and no minor folly

If the place of decision is not my own

Will my future ever be mine, and mine alone?

If not me, then who holds the reins?

What parts of myself have I too long ignored, my life disdains?

What other choices might have I made?

For how long have I been obstructed and waylaid?

And the false roads I've followed, who whispered in my ear?

Encouraging me not, rather filling me with fear

That course, the one I followed, was never meant to be mine

How many years wasted, and how much time?

That too is a question, but not one you should ask

If left unfettered, what now might be your task?

The future is yours and begins on the day

When to the past you hear yourself say

"I paid for my freedom, my life now my own

Watch now how things change because I have grown"

Is it so simple? Yes and No?

Self-aware now, there is much that is new to learn and to know

But that in itself is reason enough

To live for real and abandon the bluff.

Is it not worth a struggle to reclaim what was taken?

To discover the whole of oneself and not always be mistaken

To feel complete, free to set one's own course

It's a whole new world without guilt or remorse.

Will doubt vanish and life become sure?

Will all my acts and sentiments suddenly be pure?

Is there such a thing as a miracle cure?

To live a life that is not one's own, is not to live, but to endure

RECIPROCITY

November 2018

One morning, on my way home from walking the dogs in Central Park, I was annoyed. It was nothing major, but one of those ordinary, cumulative things that one can dismiss one at a time, only to find oneself overwhelmed with a full glass when yet another insignificant incident occurred. But are these petty slights really so insignificant, or do they reflect a larger movement which, if taken as a whole, should give cause for concern?

What happened? A lack of consideration of a motorist who is in a hurry to make the light. A dog walker whose dog has no manners and lunges at passersby and other dogs. A child who knocks into a frail older person. The potential list of insults is indeed long.

So what do they mean? One might get annoyed at just one and let it go. But cumulatively, they send a simple message: only I count, and if I bump into you, it's obviously your fault because you should has been more attentive to me. Really?

The basic psychology of the human being – from childhood through adulthood and ultimately old age – is driven by a singular process whose influence over our emotional and cognitive capacities is enormous. We start out our existence having a consciousness of only

ourselves. Parents and other caregivers come and go in a fluid, undifferentiated state of awareness First the mother, then other encountered with sufficient frequency, acquire a permanence in the child's mind. Aside from recognizing fixed objects in the external world – a major discovery if there is one – one realizes over time that they are no unlike ourselves, with the same egocentric assumptions, making for some serious learning conditions.

What saves us from this solitary state is, coming with this awareness of others, we realize the interactive nature of life. Slowly children emerge from the realm of magical thinking, and enter a concrete world where things cannot be altered by a simple thought, but that they obey certain physical laws well beyond our ability to control. This is a major concession, yet the necessary foundation of any understanding of reality.

As we become less egocentric, our consciousness begins to separate itself from the outside world, seeing itself as an independent entity interacting with an ever increasing number of others. We may call it learning, or knowledge, but the ability to see things more "objectively," i.e. independent of the old Platonic idea that something exists only if I think of it, is the very foundation of our cognitive capacities. In other words, this is how intelligence emerges from that odd place of being and non-being where all that exists is me.

The next stage involves moving away from the practical, the concrete, and to acquire the ability to speculate outcomes without having to actually experience them. In other words, as we continue to "de-centralize" the universe, we no longer need to move objects around to comprehend them. Rather, we can mentally represent them with no corporal existence, and manipulate them in any way we require towards whatever objective w may have selected. For once things have acquired their own independent existence from ourselves, we no longer need to touch them "model" them. Suddenly, the world of abstract, or formal, thinking has removed the restrictions inherent in the concrete world, and opened the door to the limitless possibilities of imagination.

Emotionally, a similar process is charted for us. The difference is that it seems to be much harder for us to evolve as reliably affectively as we can do cognitively. It is impossible to say if intelligence finds its roots in our emotions, for both function through certain organizational principals and value systems. But whereas, cognitively speaking the personality sees no threat in relativizing its own position in the world, we tend to resist every effort to reduce our relative importance to others. In other words, it is indeed one of life's challenges to evolve from a state of pure subjectivity to a place where our relative insignificance does not threaten our sense of self.

Unfortunately, the efforts we make to retain relationships on an even keep can prove wrong. Why? Because there will come a point at which the effort will no longer suffice, and even a minor infraction will provoke an inappropriately violent response.

I was aware of what was going on, and had the ability to control myself, but funny things happen when the glass is full. We begin to feel wronged, misunderstood, even maligned, often thoughtlessly or worse, unconsciously. It is no longer a minor, isolated remark, but a principle, a value, that is under attack, and rather than look to tolerance, a certain indignation seizes us, and we go from being a bit passively accepting to assertively correcting.

We may not lose control to the point of violence, though I'm certain we all have observed confrontations which have deteriorated, even among friends. Someone we knew as calm and hard to rattle suddenly is so angry that no one participating understands where this is coming from. Unless one is self-aware and could feel the tension mounting until conscious control falls away, ceding its place and role to an unconscious rage.

Without getting too lost in the weeds, the point why I mention this is because on this particular day, engaged in a pleasant conversation about current events, the others involved in the discussion began digging their heels in. Now most people nowadays are more inclined to want to speak than to listen. The is the road to frustration since even those who are rigorous in their thinking and careful to build a substantive case to make a contribution and not just to impose – at least at first – will sooner or later realize that they simply are not being heard.

 So, recognizing this as "wrong," "childish," and counterproductive, they too will begin digging in. And at this point, the conversation morphs into an argument when the substance of the discussion is no longer relevant. Only who will prevail counts, who will impose their point of view. Of the four principal resolutions there is concession, the launching of personal attacks to disqualify the speaker and thereby his arguments, a straightforward abandonment where one party just walks away, or an escalation whose limits one cannot predict.

What lies at the heart of this? There are two ways of approaching the answer. The first, and by far the least complex, is a simple rule we tend to forget, and whose place in society is essential. So essential, in fact, is that it is virtually a universal principle: It was, though declining these days, the notion that how I treat another is how I expect to be treated. Reciprocity.   It is an essential component of successful human interactions. Without it, other elemental forces take over, whose roots lie no longer in the desire to exchange information for the benefit of all, but rather a matter of only slightly sublimated rage and the thirst for power which underlies it.

Our world today has shifted from this central fulcrum role, a lodestone for balance, and a keeper of the peace, to a much more "me" centric perspective where others are, by definition (at least in my world) of lesser value than myself. If the world is seen in this way, balance becomes impossible, for the fulcrum will have shifted.

The second, more psychological in nature, relies upon the unresolved unconscious issues we tend to ignore but which are actively engaged, albeit surreptitiously, in everything we do. Prick a complex, punch a chipped shoulder, mock a bruised ego, and watch how irrational issues can ignite a fire that can consume far more than whatever was being politely discussed at the outset.

This happens all the time. The fact that we don't talk about it is because we choose not to see it. Why? To do so would require us to take an honest look at ourselves in terms of our weaknesses, our failings and flaws, our frustrated desires. It would be like asking that famous mirror from Sleeping Beauty who is the UGLIEST of all. And the answer would be me. So we defend our self image, the edited version of ourselves we offer to others, at all costs. For to do otherwise would be comparable to abandoning our goal of perfectability – however fantastical that may be – and the means by which we have successfully (to a varying degree) managed to find acceptance. It is ironic how we come to reject ourselves from our fear of rejection by others, create a mask or Persona (as Jung called it) where whatever we've been led to believe is unacceptable is denied, and to deploy enormous amounts of energy to maintain what is, essentially, an illusion.

To so identify oneself with an unattainable, unsustainable illusion can only makes us always more aware of our insecurities, require us to be constantly vigilant not to let others see the truth, and find a new constant companion in the form of anxiety--

To live off a lie is to be constantly vulnerable, never knowing where the threat may emerge, having insufficient and increasingly rigid means of defending our false selves. The end result of this dark path is self-loathing, for within us continues to live the "real" us. It cannot be silenced, or removed, but from its place in the unconscious, it will mount all sorts of protests against the injustices we commit on ourselves. We come to be at war with ourselves. It is a war both must lose, even if one seems to win.

To fear, to despise those things about ourselves we have been led to believe are flaws makes us strangers to ourselves. And whenever we feel threatened, strangers become the source of all dangers. There is but one way out of this. To see that we reality exists, it is the doman we inhabit. It obeys certain basic rules, most notably the ambition to honor what is true. Even if we can only approach the truth, we must nevertheless always seek it. It our premise is based on a lie, something by definition unreal, our chances of success decline, the further away from the truth we go.

So whenever you might feel like hating yourself, when you feel Life is punishing you for your shortcomings, stop and consider this. If Life supplies us with whatever it chooses, then this is who we are. Deny Life and she will deny you. Engage her, and you will have found the path to your full potential which alone can offer you the best chance at a real life.

One last comment about our too frequent flight into fantasy. People nowadays seem to believe that fantasy is the true expression of our desires, and that it is a responsibility, a right, to fulfill them. Nothing could be further from the truth. Fantasy is the mind's playground, its safe place to perform mind experiments, where we can explore to better understand what the unconscious is telling us in its singular language – metaphor. Take a fantasy literally if you want, but be prepared for a surprise somewhere down the road, as not all fantasies are good ones,\

It is indeed ironic that living in this country of rugged individualists, frontiersmen who fought their way across this land, have now become loud mouth bullies who will avoid a direct confrontation, preferring to snipe, or that old favorite, to criticize behind someone's back. We used to consider this a sign of an inferior character, craven and underhanded. Now, when someone intervenes, even for a just cause, people tend to slink away, not wanting to "get involved." Obviously, no one wants to get into a brawl, though these rarely happen outside certain groups. Somehow, a sense of fear, even dread, has crept into most direct confrontations, with as a result, to have rendered us less than admirable.

We tend to forget that a democratic society comes with certain obligations, one of which includes a social awareness – of oneself, of others, and of the collective whole. Take as an example If, someone intentionally or even thoughtlessly damages some public property. Whose responsibility is it to say something? Most people would say it's none of their business. But is it? Who is the public if not ourselves. If, someone damaged something of ours, would we not speak up? How is this defferent from the first example? We all own a piece of the public domain, and insofar as ownership comes with obligations, there's yet another argument in favor of intervening.

So what's gone wrong? I fear we no longer understand, and therefore fail to implement the practice of something we used to call "civic duty." It would involve such things as paying taxes, voting, going to war, obeying existing law, etc. So we abandon what is not uniquely ours, imagining that it has become now someone else's job to care for what is also mine. Really?

What's at stake here is not who throws a piece of paper on the ground, or breaks a bottle against a rock because it is fun. The matter at hand is the notion of collective responsibility, i.e. that we are all responsible for that which is held by us all. We may instruct government to accept that we delegate that responsibility for practical reasons, and authorize them to pay for such services to be delivered. But, as any owner is obligated to do, and we own the public weal, we are responsible for the properties usage and upkeep, paid for – in this instance – through our taxes or other fees.

At no point is our responsibility removed, nor, I believe, would we be pleased if someone told us that our National Parks are going to be sold off to private holdings, or appropriated by the military for their exclusive use. Why? Because it is ours, and we seem to have forgotten perhaps the very first lesson we are taught as children as we begin to interact with others: to share. As I tell my granddaughters, it's better to share because that way everyone has more. Have we become a nation of pre-schoolers?

How does this relate to the poem? I've taken a very ordinary incident, portrayed its consequences over time, and then blown it out into how it can derail the proper functioning of a democratic society such as we like to imagine ours to be. There is a collective failure of any civic sense, any notion that we are responsible in many ways for each other, and that the collective well being benefits us all, and not just the much maligned (and at time justifiable so) beneficiaries. .It has been so often stated as to be practically meaningless, but democracy requires active engagement. Government exists to advance the public good. But to ensure that it all works as it is supposed to, those whose country this is, ours, must not just embrace our entitlements (a phrase so cynically misapplied), but the responsibilities.

Imagine an individual who has decided that they owe nothing to anyone, but that others – some unidentifiable entity which is not us – owe me a comfortable, effort-free existence. They will not have set aside any funds, made plans where to live, taken care of their health capital, have health insurance, have foreseen the education of their children and their own old age – to name but a few. They will have perhaps a car, a television set, a house, furniture, etc.,etc.. All of this *seems quite normal to them, and so they are unconcerned as to how this happens and where it all comes from.*

The point I am trying to make is that every time we do something, whenever we take something for granted on the assumption that it is our due, we are stealing from the collectivity. But we forget that we all have a stake in the collectivity. And for it to function, the collectivity has the obligation to ac responsibly in the interests of all. I believe we would be hard pressed, had we asked the question cold, to find anyone who could give a clear and concise answer. And even if they did, I'm not certain the concept would be able to penetrate the protective membrane whose purpose is to maintain the primacy of themselves. There is clearly a "me". But what happened to the "us"?

Many are the adages when young we are taught

Some we forget, other were bought

Innocents and naives accept without question

No need for critiques, they cause only indigestion

A line or two to set life's course

So much reason we see there's no need for divorce

Others, on the other hand, eschew

To live by any rules, no matter how few

We call it transactional nowadays

I watch as the social fabric it frays

One example in which the logic is clear

No need for suspicion, no need for fear

Trust, of course, will always be required

Unless one day that too will be retired

True in ethics, truth in math, this idea can be applied wherever desired

But should that ever happen, we may well all have expired

So simple in concept, who could doubt?

It's the rule of reciprocity I'm talking about

As "a" does to" b" so" b" does to" a"

A balance is created, one for a long time to stay

It favors something else that we prize

We can assume both understand and embrace it as wise

But I have observed a troubling defect

That sometimes I think I am alone to detect

I used to believe that old adage could be a good guide

Nothing too fancy, just a smile warm and wide

For the most part it seemed to work well

Then mobile phones came along and it all went to hell

Like a social black hole that sucks all energy inside

No more social skills, so behind a screen they hide

Back to the Dark Ages when we didn't know we revolved around the Sun

Now I's all about me, I am the unique number one

I can walk down a street full of my kind

And see nothing, all wrapped up in my mind

Oh,excuse me, we speak now exclusively of the brain

Whoever raised these people forgot how to train

The tools of society are there to provide

A means of interaction, not a new way to hide

Where we can be whomever we want to be

There's only one problem, will anyone ever know the real me?

Even I'm not sure anymore who lives in my head

Is he alive or long ago dead?

I don't know how to reach him – hello are you still there

No matter, I never really did care

Me, I look to my buddies, or my girlfriend, better yet

She'll handle the social side, she's as good as they get

Me, I'll just live in that little world of my own

And hide out there so my real self can remain unknown

Even to me, am I overanalyzing?

This all about me thing is tantalizing

How big can I get, you've heard of rightsizing

Now some huge me could be very surprising

What am I saying:? Is that what I think?

First off I try not to do that anymore. And I need a stiff drink

Let me try again this conversational stuff

I don't really like it, I prefer to look silent and tough

A man of few words, make them think I'm cool

Gee I hope I've convinced them, I don't want to look like a fool

There it happened again – as I stepped outside

Too much thinking about things frightens me, I prefer to just hide

Now where was I? Yeah, this reciprocity thing

It's true, I've noticed people have less and less to bring

In terms of conversation, of substance , when it's not about them

After a minute or two we start counting to ten

God these people, boring, I've got so many funny stories

All serving one purpose – extolling my glories

I've got almost everything anyone could desire

It just seems, though I try, there isn't much fire

I just realized I'm happiest when it's all about me

After all, the goal of my life is to be happy

Should I care if others find me boring as hell?

Will it show and will those who've noticed tell?

Maybe if I make a list of interesting things to say

As long as I make them laugh, they'll let me stay

I'll try not to think of anything at all

And if anyone notices, I'll just try and stall

There you have it, all bundled and neat

The things that I care about go no further than my feet

Headphones on, I can feel the beat

Wait till my girlfriend finds me – is she in for a treat

Snap out of it, why does my attention continue to fail?

Am I in charge or is it that famous dog's tail?

No coherence can I find, though I rarely look

A few days ago I saw this thing about being of consequence in some random book.

It was just lying there so I picked it up fast

I don't want others to think I steal books written long ago in he
past

But wait, it was published only a month ago

Do dudes still think like this? I didn't know

Wow , does he have his head up his ass

It gave me a headache, so on the rest I took a pass

His point, I think, was we've gotten way out in front

Of ourselves, he says we're lost – now that's blunt

All we know is how to count to know the value of things

He also says that counting no happiness brings

After he says we consume too much stuff

And he asks if anyone knows when enough is enough

There are too many people squeezing blood from a stone

Sooner than later we'll be here all alone

No animals, no trees, the oceans will be bare

God, how will I know what to wear?

Then he goes on and talks about this thing left behind

It's called courtesy and how it's important to be kind

What the fuck – what does that mean?

Acting that way won't steal any scene

And those animals, all furry and cute

God put them here for us to eat – who can refute?

The Church says they're dumb, they're not smart like us

So it's totally cool to throw then all under the bus

OK, I haven't thought this much since I can't recall

One more heavy thought and my hair will start to fall

I've always been told He will see to our needs

After all, we're just like Him and come from his seeds

What Father would let his kids ruin a good deal?

Shit – no way – guilty he'd feel

So I'll just think about what to do today

And things will be cool as long as Mom and Dad continue to pay

I've gone to school, gotten my degree

What more do they want, I'm tired, from me

They taught me to take, only fools give back

So off I go cause I'm sure I'm on the right track

THE GUARDIAN

September 2018

A recent friendship brought many similar experiences from the past back to life, and with it, clarity as to what was really happening. This poem was written from the heart and not the head, as the best one's often are. How do I know? I started writing this same introduction to it, and four pages later, found myself lost in my own explanations, trying to substantiate every point, lead the reader to my own conclusions, rather than let them feel the message, rather than understand it. As always, I am amazed at how much simpler, clearer, more meaningfully things can be expressed when we just get out of our own way.

For those who don't see it that way, let me nevertheless try and provide some context. This most recent friendship began, as the best ones do, because they were meant to. It was not some role to or part to play, but rather two parts of an equation, interacting in the most spontaneous, natural way. Equations rarely resolve themselves, but do contain the components of their solution, leaving it up to us to find it.

For anyone who has read any of my previous writings, though perhaps most explicitly in Mr. Hide's Progress and then The Leftovers of God's Anger, not all energy is devoted to a solution. The past, with all its bad compromises, has taken years to refine its voice, defend its position, often from a time when it actually represented the best possible solution to a difficult situation.

The problem is, life goes on, the equations evolve along with their requirements. Unfortunately, those pas answers tend to calcify, taking on a life of their own. And with that, rather than helping, they become through their conviction that they continue to be essential, they become impediments.

These are not just abstract constructs, but have become entities with personalities of their own, and prime directives endowed with a sense of mission and considerable strength. Call them by some other name if it helps – defenses, rationalizations, delusions or denials. I prefer to see them in their totality – almost as alter egos, for that is how they see themselves. They are the Guardians from the past who will always fail to recognize their current irrelevance, and worse.

Should the reasons for their existence remain, their obstinate refusal to cede their place to newer, more progressive, more helpful answers grows. And grows. Until they come to see the hopeful person as betraying themselves, requiring these Guardians to perceive those they are supposed to protect as much the enemy as the friend pointing a way forward.

In extreme situations, and there are many more than we imagine, for this phenomenon exists in a multitude of forms, the Guardians redirect *their efforts against the person trying to change, and more specifically, against the friend who is acting as a catalyst for change. The first step is ambivalence, where the person sways back and forth between the Guardian, the past, and the Friend, the future. This ebb and flow, this "one step forward, one step back," is exhausting and confusing, raising the stakes always higher. Until the Guardian actually replaces the person, confirming the ways of the past, and the voice of the Friend and their own future, is silenced.*

It is a sad thing to participate in, but too often, it is inevitable, given the weight of the past and the fear only the Guardian has been able to defy – so far. Fear, or its more diffuse cousin, anxiety, are figments of the mind, only as strong as they go unconfronted. Once drawn into the light, we begin to see them for who they are, where they came from, and how those demons are only little elves, enlarged by their distance from the light, rendered more frightening as insubstantial shadows. These are the things that frighten children – and that is the problem.

Courage is not the absence of fear. It is the awareness of fear but confronted for some higher purpose.

It takes tremendous courage to let go of the past and step into the unknown. But courage is something we are meant to develop as we grow. It is not an innate quality. But today, courage is a little understood and less valued thing than it once was. Which is why we live in a world overpopulated by children, children of all ages, with all the consequences we are only now coming to realize.

Is there hope? I believe there is always hope that one day, after however long the person has lived in the shadows, a rebellion will overturn the repressive regime, destroy the prison, and set the person free from their past. Am I optimistic? If I look to experience, I should say no. But then, that would not be me. So I write this for those who live in the dark shadows of their own prisons of the past. That they may look first for their courage, for that is the very first step towards freedom.

For those who grow up unprotected

With neither parents nor another self-selected

To shield a child from assaults unfounded

Unless one looks to the assailant grounded

The one who has an axe to grind

And the hand that wields it from their unconscious mind

Believing themselves to be well intended

While delivering blows that will go unmended

Severing parts from the original whole

Unaware of their selfish goal

For sons born of mothers with wounds of their own

Loving their sons in ways that deny they've grown

From boys to men, to assume their place

The scars go deep but leave no visible trace

Unless one looks to the choices they make

One after another, each successive mistake

One step, an affirmation

To be followed by an equivalent negation

The same holds true, though in other ways

Fathers too deny their daughters happier days

They should provide an image of man as protector and shield

Instead, heavy handed they frighten, and force to yield

Rather than choose the difference to embrace

What should be welcome will now wear a menacing face

Variations exist though the path is the same

Some solution must emerge, what will be its name?

I call it the Guardian, I've seen it revealed

And how by its hand a fate is sealed

From out of the shadows, its mission clear

To create another that knows no fear

It takes years to form, a life of its own

Until one day, its face is shown

As yielding by day, that fierce by night

It knows no retreat, accepts no flight

Its mission, to protect, a compromise enabled

Unless required, it lives quietly stabled

Watching its host struggle to be free

To reclaim a wholeness and its liberty

But the dragon's voices won't let go

And the child within fears to never say no

Life goes on, though the path is wrong

Daily is sung the family's poisonous song

To deny each initiative, calling to come back home

Freedom is hard when carrying such a heavy stone

The years go by, the movement stalls

And then begins a series of falls

In fiction, in fact, the road continues to narrow

The harm is real, the prospect too harrow

A friend arrives, tries to assist

An ebb and flow takes shape, an opportunity missed

The Guardian grew strong as the host grew weak

Arrogant and assured, a language of lies does it speak

"No need have I for help, my life is mine,

Its way forward I alone will define"

With no warning we ask what's become of the host?

Where once he was real, he's now a ghost

Without seeing it happen, their places exchanged

Will he rise again, or will he remain forever enchained?

Each man a dragon must he slay

The question is, will he choose his someday?

Where will the required courage be found?

Will he ever learn to truly stand his ground?

Will it be enough to change his mind?

His way in this world will he ever find?

Lost in the din, he must find his voice

Then use it - the essential choice.

WHO IS AMERICAN?

September 2018

I wrote this during the immigration crisis when the Trump administration began its policy of separating those immigrants trying to enter the United States from their children. Obviously, this was not only a terribly inhumane policy but one for which no preparation had been undertaken. It was not a surprise coming from the President, but I as surprised the speed at which is was willingly implemented by those called upon to execute it. Reminiscent, yes, of Nazi Germany, when the common soldiers did what they were told without questioning their orders, I had thought this type of excuse had been disqualified. But like the Germans and other collaborators at the time, policies such as these reflect a profound prejudice, an unreasonable fear, and even a desire among some to either exact revenge on the offending peoples or simply enjoy the rush of being able to dominate other human beings they have suddenly been authorized to feel superior to. It is an example of our basest emotions which we may deny, even condemn. But under the right circumstances, when the moral guard rails have been removed, it can and will rear once again its ugly face.

Coming back to the issue of who is American, given the colonization or this country and the systematic efforts to eliminate those who had lived here for hundreds, if not thousands of years before the arrival of the Europeans, I thought it not only worthwhile, but necessary to recall the facts of our history in a way that perhaps we will be less able to dismiss. The oral tradition, in the form of poems, often lends itself better than linear prose, to getting past the rationalization we so easily concoct.

This is not a matter of trying to elicit a sense of guilt, for that is what those who perpetrate such acts fear most, and defend against the most aggressively. As Jung said:

> "We cannot change anything until we accept it.
> Condemnation does not liberate, it oppresses"

The only way to break through is to elicit an empathetic response, draw those who refuse to actually feel what these people were put through, robbed of, and abandoned to our forgetfulness.

We are all immigrants here, many of us may even have come here illegally. And that is wrong. But that does not mean we should or can shut the door. Enormous mistakes have been made in the past which reflect more our greed and shortsightedness than those values we proclaim to the world. If we do not live by them, whatever the response, we cannot claim them. We are what we do. Not what we say.

I recall a conversation I had with some Swiss people on my arrival. They asked me very matter of factly why Americans were such racists. This was in the very early 1970s, not long after riots had rocked many cities, crime was on the rise, and there were few things restraining the accumulated hostility between the races. Having lived through the decades prior, I had seen a rapid migration of black and Hispanics which had shocked the current inhabitants. On an individual level, there was never a problem, as two people can, if so inclined, find a way to get along. It was a group phenomenon, and one of the speed at which the migration had occurred.

So I asked my Swiss friends the status of their foreign population. Interestingly, as a foreign student, I was put through the rather humiliating process migrant workers were subjected to. It was useful, for my awareness was based on experience, and experience is the path to empathy. I knew the answer before I had asked the question. There were extremely strict rules designed to limit the number of foreigners, to ensure that Switzerland remained for the Swiss with severe limitations on the acquisition of property, the difficulties erected to discourage the acquisition of citizenship, and so on. The point is not to criticize the Swiss, but to demonstrate how quickly we can embrace a moral blindness which shields us from our own inconsistencies.

By the way, this last point, our ability to embrace blindness where convenient, is a theme you will certainly recognize elsewhere.

One observation on race, which has become something of a catchall for problems of immigration – often confusing it – I think race may be a superficial marker, but it is not the cause. I believe the problem is the confrontation of cultures, and he's one way of looking at it.

Imagine you are a foreigner recently arrived in a host country. A local person invites you to their home for dinner. You accept because they represent something you admire and respect and aspire to become a member of. In essence, you are a guest and have come because you want to belong. However, to join, to be consistent with the concept of the guest/host relationship, there is an unstated requirement. And that requirement is to assimilate. If a guest comes to your home and then insists on maintaining their culture in a way which puts it in conflict with your own – intentionally or not – is an affront, a rejection, and potentially an assault on local culture.

It is not an answer to claim for oneself, as a guest, the rights of freedom without the responsibilities of respect. The inconsistency should be obvious. Why come to my home, the place you say you want to live, yet you bring the culture of the place you want to flee.

Of course, there will be nostalgia for the good things left behind, but one must never forget why one left in the first place, and why one chose the destination one did. Three of my four grandparents were immigrants, coming when they were teenagers. In all the years I knew them, I never heard them once mention where they came from, or try to recreate what they were glad to have left. From the moment they set foot here, there were Americans and never looked back. And their children were the same.

Immigration is a choice. It may be made under extreme duress, but that does not exonerate anyone from the responsibilities inherent in *assimilating. That doesn't mean on rejects and denies one's national origins or culture. It does mean that there are obligations due the host country. Those immigrant groups who simply recreate their home country culture in their host country are planting a foreign body into the local population. This is, by definition an irritant, and when that happens, the body responds by attacking to foreign body. At least that's how biology handles it.*

Societies have immune systems just like bodies. They may be irrational, unfair, and even cruel. But to deny them is to invite conflict. It is time to set aside the racial shorthand, and begin examining the real problems. Migrating cultures are under stress and often experience periods of regret at having left their homes. This is natural. But like any guest, and like any host, hospitality must be the rule. Both sides have responsibilities and for this to succeed, both must live up to their obligations to each other.

When talk about who is American, of whom do we speak?

Of the strong, the brave, the shy or the meek?

Of those who come from another place?

With another belief, another race?

Or in silence, who is it we really see?

That depends, of course, if our minds are free

For America is neither a race nor a creed

In the same way all comers from their past were freed'

The founding fathers came mostly from a privileged class

Many others we poor, ignorant and crass

We think of them as Christian, white and good

It's time we took a look under the hood

There were slaves of course, but they didn't count

And the vast majority arrived with but a paltry amount

The true Americans, those who were here first

Got treated so cruelly and got off the worst

America, in fact, is an idea, not a race

To be an American by birth no past can erase

One could declare those who came by choice

Worked hardest to succeed and should retain the loudest voice

That too would be wrong, missing the fact

To be an American there's a way one must act

If an idea lies at the root of it all

From this idea our ideas flow as if from a waterfall

Rich in quantity, pure in intent

Ancestors came here to own, not to rent

To build a nation of values, not the whims of some king

To shine a light in this world, something better to bring

So those who legally may be Americans by right

Too should be required to earn the privilege before launching
some fight

Are their actions reflective of those values which define this
nation?

Or have they deformed now and turned them into a myth, a lie,
a false creation?

If we no longer act as we said we should

Then the values have gone from gold to wood

We've become another people, no better than any other

All that remains of the idea is greed and money, our souls to
smother

It's clear we have strayed from who we claim to be

Though we talk of freedom and liberty

That all men are equal – or so we say

As long as they look like me, that's the only way

If this is the only criteria we're willing to support

Then the idea is gone, the mission ready to abort

So stop thinking you're American if you act otherwise

You're not, don't you see, so open your eyes.

THANK GOD FOR OUR GUNS
June 2018

After yet another mass shooting I began to wonder how it was that we felt such a need for guns. I can imagine, if those Westerns provided a faithful representation of the past, that living out alone on the prairie, beyond the reach of the law, one had to know how to protect oneself. After all, the Indians, the wolves, the outlaws were all out there in the dark waiting for an opportunity to kill us as we slept.

Obviously, this description is a bit tongue and cheek, but I wonder how much this myth we have created of ourselves has not laid a foundation for our gun culture. For essentially, the only reason I can find for wanting a gun, mental health issues aside, is because one is afraid and feels incapable, with his natural means, to defend himself. But then I asked myself if I walk the city in fear, if I am always vigilant, on the lookout for some shadowy presence waiting to pounce.   And the answer was no.

How many of us, and I am not denying that danger does exist, have actually experienced a situation where a gun would have helped? Since rational beings usually base their perceptions on experience, and the statistics suggests that it is more dangerous to have a gun then not to have one when confronted with a violent individual, why then this fascination? I'm afraid the answer is that for reasons which have little to do with external realities, a significant number of people live in fear. If the fears are not based in reality, then on what are they based?

 Small children go through a period between 3 and 5 when they have nightmares of wild animals, mythical creatures, or in Europe, it's often the Gypsies who will come in the night and kidnap small children. Obviously, these are manifestations of the unconscious where the conscious mind is attempting to come to terms with these primal images which live in the shadows.   They are frightening because children can't really defend themselves. So they run to their parents for protection.

The infamous "bogey man" is another representation of something we don't understand and therefore fear. His vocation of lurking in the shadows waiting to frighten us apparently does not disappear at the age of 5. For these fears which many adult gun lovers maintain are of this order. Rather, they are cultural artifacts from another time whose relevance has passed. Unfortunately, we have created something of a chicken and egg situation, for it the bogey man has a gun, I need one too. But if he wants to take what is mine, then he will need a bigger gun. An escalation – all on the level of fantasy – ensues until the imagined threat has assumed such proportions that reason has abandoned us.

Erase all traces of the evil we have done

Wrap it up in Jesus, and the lies we have spun

In his name some feel all there is should be theirs

The winner takes all, for the loser who cares?

How long can this last, has the Devil claimed Jesus' throne?

He promises to absolve us of our sins, so no need to atone

All this is done in His holy name

Take all that we want, we've but to claim

This land created by men of wealth for the most part

in a time of Enlightenment, reason before heart

They thought to banished the darkness from men's souls

With a piece of paper that enshrined these goals

Originalists, Evangelicals, those who proclaim their love of the

Constitution

Have forgotten the cruelty with which we deployed destitution

Like some fig leaf they cry Freedom and individual rights

But instead of reason, they seem to prefer the fights

 How manly are they, these protectors of liberty

These are real men, no time for understanding or empathy

We've a nation to build and wars to fight

Proudly we marched off into the dark night

 Safe from all fear, take not our guns away

For the second amendment we will fight every day

No need to think or ask ourselves why

What do I so fear that others must die?

Are there Indians circling my cabin, hungry for blood?

Are there immigrant criminals covered in mud?

Are there dark skinned men here to rape our wives?

Are they all carrying razor blades and knives?

Or maybe the danger is less real, I can't find its source

Might it come from within us, whispers of an evil course?

Does the government truly seek to take all that is mine?

With their corrupt agendas, though high values they opine

After all, what's mine I've acquired alone

Really? Do you live on some bountiful island as yet unknown?

Where the roads were there when you arrived

And the schools and the hospitals and the fields – as if by magic

they thrived

And the armed forces, there always to protect

On the lookout for our real enemies on the ready to detect

Have we lost all sense of perspective and proportion together?

Should we not also fear aliens, agnostics and the weather?

What a world to inhabit if everything is reasons for fear

Our insecurities enraged, no reason can we see or hear

Could it be some fantasy based on our myths, but deformed?

Have we created a new religion, White Christianity, Reformed?

Where inspired by the past, for those were the days

When we were all white and Christian with our righteous ways

When it was normal to keep others down

To chase those not like us out of town

 To make them live far away from our homes

So we could be safe – but wait, were they really gnomes?

The ones who abandon their minds and their souls

For us alone should be reserved our lofty goals

Believing these others are less than we, the blessed

I think by now my point you will have guessed

For I see in this nation a soul full of contradiction

Some of our values are real, others have now become fiction

Empowered we are, all hail to me

For I want to live among only the brave and the free

To hell with the others, they poison our race

They can't say it yet, if only we could eliminate their trace

Or at least to be sure they know their place

To live by ourselves – may it be so by His holy grace

Beyond racism, beyond creed, we are a self-righteous breed

We alone have the right on this bounteous land to feed

To rape and despoil it, to be rich today

To hell with those tree loving regulators, who cares what they
say

Tomorrow will take care of itself as it has always done

We live in the present, so let's just have fun

With no regard for anything but how much we earn

Too many stand by passively, as our future we burn

It's not too late, for the day is long

To stand up for this land where all creatures have a right to

belong

None here on God's Earth the truth can they claim

To do so is a coward's way and on the rest a vile stain

If we be men, reason should prevail

If we rely on dumb faith we can only fail

Not some beliefs from a time when men lived in a tent

Only the ignorant embrace what's given without thoughtful

time spent

Reflecting not just on grandiose ideas

Simple thoughts too can bring humility, not primitive fears

These guns we need to protect from enemies we fear though

they reamin unseen

Is that what makes us so uncaring, so greedy, so mean?

Is not the demon we fear more the one living inside?

Drag him into the sunlight and you might no longer have to hide

Imagine a world where you can walk without fear

And not depend on always having a sidearm near

When you could look at others and engage with a smile

You might be surprised if we all gave it a trial

Ask yourself what does God have to do with gun rights?

Are we really his choice, the Protector, to win all the fights?

Or rather is this Lord the one of Peace?

Would that He free us from fear, and our hearts release

If of God one wishes to speak, do so alone

I'm certain there are other sins for which you could atone

Religion is not a fig leaf behind which to hide

Rather by its precepts we should try and abide

Don't rally the faithful, don't speak of exception

Take a hard look at yourself and start changing direction.

THE HERO

September 2018

When I wrote this poem I was obviously both frustrated and upset. The world, it seemed was filled with those who closed their eyes, ran from the challenge, wanting only one thing – that someone else would come along to fix what was broken.   I found this perplexing for a country that insists on its own exceptionalism, its innovation, and the often unstated assumption that, by definition, it is the first among all others.

But something happened along the way as we came to identify with only part of our history while ignoring the cost to others. We lost the always necessary perspective of our historical purpose along on our successful journey to material success. As even achievements come with a dark side, without perspective, arrogance takes hold and humility recedes. One could speculate that the last great progressive push dates from the JFK/Johnson era. After that, we settled in, grew self-satisfied, even entitled, and failed to notice what was happening to our moral fiber, our character. With the 1980s began the Era of Entitlement, Self-Centeredness and Greed.

Interestingly, there were reactions, however misguided they may have been. The emergence of a resurgent fundamental Christianity brought forth a very un-Christian, rigid, even punitive moral code. Supported by a blind faith in Capitalism – itself a very individualistic, competitive based system where the winners have a higher moral value than the "losers," whose condition is the result of their own moral laxity. Following on from the wild 1960s and 1970s where every convention was challenged, and casual overtook formality, it is not surprising that in parallel, from one country, we became two. Life is complicated enough without a fundamental duality, and incompatible opposition of values which alienated the middle while reinforcing the two extremes. This confusing state had profound effects on the psychology of many in our society as confusion is a deeply anxiogenic condition, particularly for those barely able to compete in our rather heartless system.

There are two fundamental schools of thought in the academic historical world regarding great men and the role they play in events. One is called the "Great Man Theory" which states that exceptional individuals will rise out of the mass by dint of their own qualities. The other is more the idea that events come together to create opportunities where individuals who might otherwise lead ordinary lives, are drawn into position of great influence. Though I am no fan of equivocation, in many instances, both are true.

Though no one truly saw the current situation coming before it was here, hindsight can often help inform our present, and if we are wise enough, help shape our future. Perhaps more importantly than the 1960s, the 1980s brought about a fundamental conservative revolution which had been in preparation since the defeat of Barry Goldwater in 1964. Seeing their influence declining, a new strategy emerged as a polar opposite to the Democratic agenda.

Ronald Reagan said it best: The government is not the solution to the problem. It is the problem. With that was born an anti-government ethos, supported by a systematic mischaracterization of the role of the federal government. Coinciding with the Viet Nam debacle, the race riots, the inflation challenge of the 1970s, and the stalling of the economy, the country was ripe and ready to find someone, or *something, to blame. The federal government was the ideal target. And Ronald Reagan was the man to carry the message. Rather than the dour and too serious Jimmy Carter, here was a man who, in a lesser version of FDR, who projected affability, optimism, strength and conviction. His message was simple, and not dissimilar to that of the current President – MAGA – to which one could substitute Make America White, Christian, with Small town values, anti-immigrant, and all about business. America first.*

Deregulation is the answer to undo the labyrinth of federal rules and regulations which make us too expensive, too uncompetitive, too permissive and too indulgent. The enemy came from within. It was the "bad us" that was giving away the store. We had to defeat them and their Godless leftwing ideas and policies if we were to essentially turn back the clock to another, earlier, more innocent era which existed mostly in the minds of those who chose to believe, rather than to know.

What does this have to do with the hero, the subject of this poem? It is a historical evocation of how, to paraphrase Harry Truman,"…in a democracy, the people get the government they deserve." Though it may appear to be something of a testy dismissal, it contains certain essential elements required in any successful democracy.

Democracy is based on a few basic assumptions, perhaps the most important being the requirement of an educated, well informed and engaged electorate, for it is they who decide. Some far off Washington DC becomes the enemy only when the people who these politicians represent have grown to be self-satisfied, complacent, ignorant by choice, greedy through their own lack of a meaningful value system they have consciously understood and embraced, inhabited by an avidity since the choices made in no way respond to the spiritual and intellectual vacuum which has come to exist.

As a society based on speed, convenience, and profit, we have emptied ourselves of any trace of real curiosity. Since we are the best, where is there left to go? Binary, superficial, incurious, short-term focused, anxious and materialistic, we no longer know who we are. And that indeed is a terrible state of affairs, both as individuals and as a nation – for we must never forget, the nation is not someone else we can blame. The nation is a collection of individuals who, like it or not, together constitute the mindset of a nation.

The leaders any nation chooses reflect a collective consciousness which cannot be denied as existing and functioning. When I attempt to introduce this notion into any conversation, the immediate reaction is defensive, itself a reflection of the current malaise. The final proof is the President we have elected. This man is a caricature of who we have become – vain, selfish, transactional, fearful, greedy, lacking totally in perspective and empathy. He is our hero, at least for part of the country. And if we refuse to acknowledge ourselves in him, however much we may say we don't like him, then change will come with great difficulty.

Real change can happen only when we embrace as our own what is wrong because we have acknowledged to ourselves that things are not right. Denial of a factual situation, of reality, is to embrace fantasy. The former is where we live. The latter is where we retreat to when we don't want to acknowledge reality. Be it individual or society as a whole, any attempt to live a fantasy can only fail because it does not see clearly. The Nazi experiment is a perfect example. We may claim to be better. No doubt we are. But the trap is the same, and if we fall into it, we will create our own version of hell.

This poem is about each one of us seeking the hero within us all. Too many, expecting to be perfect but fearing the opposite, hide behind a wall of denial when a mirror is what is needed. Supporting an illusion, version of reality, and not our own reality, requires huge expenditures of energy with very little payment. It is a prime terrain for anxiety with the concurrent search for remedy – one way of approach the extent of drug abuse in our society – thereby worsening the initial situation.

Weakness is embraced as an excuse rather than courage as a way forward. If too few believe they can actually have an impact, there will be none. This is not some New Age call to arms for it promises nothing but a return to what is real. Do we really need who sells us fantasies from the past? Or do we need someone who incarnates those qualities required of a hero – courage, honesty, integrity and a belief in their own ability to change, if not the world, why not start with oneself?

"HERO IS A VERB, NOT A NOUN"

The Hero is one who is born to know

That to be alive is to always grow

Not in wealth or power or influence

But to have a vision that transcends the present tense

To know there is more than just me

If some are enslaved then none are free

Those by system, by law unfair

One thought there is, how do they dare?

But for those who by choice wear a chain

There is no pardon nor right to complain

Nor hide behind the shrouds of the weak

If by choice then they have no right to speak

For the key is there, the lock doesn't exist

Nothing binds them by leg or wrist

Weakness is chosen by default, easier it seems

Reality is too hard so they retreat into dreams

For that is the place where there is but one rule

Live there too long and become a tool

This world is harsh and comes with no guarantee

We have eyes to look, and minds to see

Mistakes abound as their lessons are true

Build on them and take their cue

To claim perfection is to espouse a lie

Sterile and lame, never ask why

It's the parent of ignorance with many a child

None with a future, living out of control, wild

To live in the present is to be its captive

Inhabited only be take, a stranger to give

For the present is gone the instant it's there

In that case for certain, why bother to care?

Without care we live behind our own wall

Starve a heart and it will stall

And what of our problems, they don't just go away

Who believes it will work if we simply turn away?

What a vision of life, is that our ambition?

Full speed ahead to our own demolition?

Like children we clamor for a leader to come

They will know how to fix things and bring back the Sun

All we have to do is await their arrival

And thus will be ensured our collective survival

Oh so we believe? Is that how you think?

How long will we wait, and get how close to the brink?

Is there still time, should panic set in?

Oh God, won't someone save us from our chosen sin?

The one hope I see, the only one in fact

Is if we wake up from this nightmare and begin to act

Starting with ourselves, to see who we've become

To work together and forget the insanity of the gun

Whose only purpose is to kill and maim

Lord what a curse on this earth we are, what a stain

For there used to reside in each and every one

The kernel of a hero, not someone just looking for fun

The one who sees beyond their own avidity

In whom is rekindled the desire to be free

Neither to envy, nor blame nor to conspire

Someone who can look above and beyond and aspire

To be better instead of having just more

One who knows that life holds wonders in store

Not easy to find nor for anyone to possess

Whose courage fears not to look at our mess

Instead of seeing challenges beyond our pale

Welcome the chance to confront the gale

Not to defeat but some measure to gain

Of what they can do when unwilling to wane

Success will come but not every day

There is room for failure to learn a new way

The journey is said to be worth more than any destination

Turn away from the past and find the road to salvation

CAUGHT

YouTube is a funny thing. There are so many reasons to go there and look. I don't go that often, but when I do it is to share some of those artists and songs who have touched me deeply. My tastes can be varied, but the choices are always individual and personal. I may start with Beverly Sills, move on to Barbra Streisand, Linda Ronstadt, John Denver to name but a few. But I always end up at the same place.

Joni Mitchell's 200 rendition of Both Sides Now. She has, of course, aged, her sprightly young voice has weathered many storms, and her dysrythmic body, moving somewhat out of synch with her perfectly in touch voice remain. But here is a person whose authenticity is striking, all the more so as she sings, with a very different meaning, perhaps her most famous song. One can only sense how much she has lived, reflected on her life, expressed the experiences she has shared with other and those she has borne alone. She says she really doesn't really know love – or life – at all. I would so beg to differ.

Each time I hear this song, it moves me, for she in these moments, and perhaps in others, more private, she is so very real. Does one feel respect, admiration, the dignity that comes from a life lived with as much sincerity as any one person can muster? Do I feel all of those things at the same time? Or do I share somehow, and in spite of her denials, the answers she has found?

I came of age with her, shared some of her music, though not all, but am a child of the 60s, with all the promise, change, learning and mistakes – and now look at the direction of the world more in disappointment than admiration. Perhaps that's why her sincerity, her authenticity mean so much.

She is not an icon. She is not a role model. She is not a star or a celebrity. There is so much wisdom in her art, so much searching, so much pain and loss, all paid in the service of Life and its requirements. Yet Life has shown her how to be real. That can be a heavy, solitary burden for anyone to bear – possibly most difficult for one so adored for reasons not always consonant with those she might embrace.

I speak in terms of being caught, of not finding easy answers or rewards for living in a way most consequential with my North Star. There is, of course, a sadness. But the bitterness some might see is tempered with a sense of coherence, of groundedness, of a questioning certainty, that bring their own consolation.

Perhaps to live thusly means to live alone. Not because one is better than anyone else, or more deserving, or undeserving for that matter. But because Life is itself a contradiction, where the most sincere, the most caring, find not some pot of gold at the end of the rainbow, but themselves. Is that not perhaps the true answer to the question?

I am not done yet, I have a hunger for life and the experiences it offers. I will continue to search, knowing yet not knowing at the same time. The former helps me avoid making the same mistakes as I have in the past. The latter keeps me moving forward.

My answer – provisional at present, but in the right direction. I try and share it in the hope that others, those who haven't found their own North Star and have given up the search for it, or those who simply don't believe that such a thing exists, may feel a spark inside their souls that just might reignite a fire that should never have been allowed to die.

I don't think anyone can answer these questions for another. What I can do, what I believe anyone can do if they are so inclined, is shine a light, point the way, engender courage, and rejoice as others look up again at the night sky to find their own North Star. Personally, I can't imagine life without it. But that's just me.

PART I

A life spent in trying to find

The secret door into my mind

The one that leads to that which I seek

I've got a sense, the occasional peek

Was it always the same?

Though it never spoke its name

Since I've been free to pursue this quest

I've taken risks and given it my best

But it seems that since I left my past life

The one with a family, a house and a wife

Not one initiative has lasted beyond a short time

Though I don't think the fault was in the normal sense mine

For I come from a place where I lived as child number two

So I settled for less, that's what I knew

No anger, no resentment, my nature seemed satisfied

I became self sufficient, on myself I relied

Of course not immune, there was a price unsuspected

Only later was that chip on my shoulder was detected

Nothing unique here, we all have a cross of our own

We see the consequences, only the origin is unknown

Until it's there, looking into our eyes

No longer is it possible to sustain the same lies

So off I went, good fortune watched over me

In a land of constraint I learned to be free

No one knew me or the baggage I brought

The web of limitations in which I'd been caught

Those voices reminding me to be afraid

Their ropes holding me back had now grown frayed

My life now my own, I would no longer be delayed

No desire for revenge, in this place I stayed

I'd found myself, more sure I would know

When I found this land where I could grow

Doubt I knew, in a form unique

Answers appeared before I could speak

I found I could see where others were blind

Hungry to learn, wanting to speak my mind

Reactions varied, at times standing part

Others were drawn to me as a place to start

No choice had I but to listen to my heart

Now, it seemed, the horse was in tune with the cart

For I knew more than most how to care

My confidence flowed from a source fresh and fair

I gave because I knew there was much to give

It seemed natural to me, free now myself to live

Not to possess others, to direct or control

More to light a path to their own way to be whole

Those who came were more than a few

I shared unsparingly whatever I knew

But in the end, we stood at the line

The one would have to cross, no longer to resign

The courage I'd shared and tried to impart

It was a place for a brand new start

One simple step was all that was needed

Had my words be heard, the counsel heeded

I'd beckon, encourage, in every way I knew

But those who truly wanted more proved to be very few

Had I been mistaken, a sin for which I should atone

Did this new place exist for real or some imaginary zone?

To look in the mirror, the truth to seek

If one will not listen, the truth will not speak

The question is not whether or not I am right

Though now I can sense those who lives in the day or the night

A quest this Is, no simple affair

The leave the past behind, one must dare

The prison offers familiarity

And even a reassuring security

No matter if the walls are thick and high

And one can no longer see the open sky

There are guards who protect, or so it might seem

Challenge their role and they will grow mean

For they have one purpose, one alone

To hold you inside though there be but one sin to atone

I see now why in those ill at ease

In whom fear is the primal disease

Feelings the enemy, safe the best friend

If so, what kind of message would such a life send?

More alone than me, empty of care

Without the courage to desire nor need to be fair

To search in the darkness, sniffing the ground

How would one know if it was ever to be found?

To fear the unknown, a future at odds with their past

Even if they've lived life hungry, as in a fast

Deprived of the sustenance they might have otherwise known

A pall now settled on field where they;ve sown

A wintery season, the growth cycle interrupted

Neither belief nor hope to contradict the process thusly corrupted

Together we may walk to the line of hope

All they need do is to cut the rope

I might as well ask them to scale a great height

In a terrible storm, on the darkest night

Or to swim the ocean with sharks infested

Little matter, they refuse to be tested

How else to discover one's true capacity

Without that knowledge, power is but a fantasy

To know that to fall means we must once again rise

That's how it works on the road to wise

But me, who has tackled challenges beyond the norm

No hero in fact, though I've weathered many a storm

I sought my destiny with demons to slay

And to my past I decreed I am me and I am here to stay

For to fail oneself is the worst sin of all

To dither and lie only to forestall

When the commitment made so long ago

Was to embrace one's sentence, freedom never to know

I seem to draw those of this mind

Who see a promise that's strong and kind

But they are fooling themselves, too afraid to be free

Their hearts are denied and their dreams empty

My eyes are now open, there is clarity

I know deception when I see

I may be strong, but one cannot convince

Someone committed their own courage to evince

Having learned now when to call it a day

Before it's the other who runs away

We all have our history, it's who we are

But choices there are as to just how far

It's as simple as that, and just as hard

Not everyone draws the wild card

Luck plays a role, but it's not alone

We all much choose, to rent or to own

This is what I come to know

There is a price, even to grow

More stay behind than forge ahead

There isn't that much time before we are dead

So I continue my path, there is no choice

And I speak what I know, having now a clear voice

If I am of those meant to walk alone

Then that is how it will be for my Life I will own

No deep sadness or guilt plagues my day

I have taken my place and here will I stay

Planting seeds wherever, perhaps to one day find a home

This is all one can do – be clear and be known

Though at time I tire of this search without end

It gets harder to believe in what might wait around the next bend

I don't know how to surrender, to lay down my arms

I have too much to give and life has too many charms

PART II

Can life be that cruel that she sets us a task?

One we didn't seek nor for which did we ask

For a riddle, a joke, with an ending unclear

Were I to resign would await only darkness I fear

I live for the light, it lives within me

It defines everything and all that I see

Others don't care to look, to feel as I do

Why at ease with our feelings are we so few?

I seem to speak a language foreign and strange

The words that I hear seem often to derange

I see what I see, that I cannot change

So the rest I leave to Life to arrange

Yet I see them as a light pointing the way

Like gifts for which there is no price to pay

But it seems to me those myths of old

Where heroes were rewarded with beauties and fleece of gold

Took time, arriving perhaps at an age when I'm old'

An empty tale have I been sold?

At times in a vicious circle, in a web of light am I caught

I've tried all I know, many demons have I fought

But my kind of freedom has not found its place

Nor a heart, nor a soul, nor a friend, nor a face

Is this the price I have had to pay

To see clearly and be able to say

To defend a truth I know to be real

Not just for me, but so all can feel

Neither fear nor envy nor self-limitation

Nor shame nor sadness nor humiliation

A perfect world have I imagined, a fantasy of my own?

From some alienation has an illusion grown?

My answer did not come without trials, more numerous than I
care to recall

I am no better than any other, on my way I've known many a fall

I know when a lie is approaching to cloud my view

I have come to know that what is shiny is not often new

I know the past, perhaps better than most

The hinterland and not just the coast

I've had my heart broken in many ways

And yet it lives, and here it stays

Life is a struggle, I deserve no special grace

Yet I long to share what remains in a warmer place

With someone who sees me not for what I can provide

Who hears their own voices with each stride

Who know their own light and fear it not

Who believe they can always alter their own plot

Who want another, a partner, together to face the storm

Who have found their way, and ignore the norm

Who have unearthed the courage not just to live

But with riches untold in their hearts to give

I think of Ulysses, so many years was he lost

With challenges many, often paying a great cost

Though nothing came with either grace or ease

With conviction not doubt, his future to seize

What would he have done if he never made it home?

Where is the myth that ends with the hero alone?

Do these stories exist only to inspire?

Can the flames burn forever that much higher?

Is the answer there waiting, being its own prize?

Is that what it means through the years to grow wise?

A riddle, a clue, another fork In the road

Does the mystery endure so as to goad?

Onward and upward with no endpoint in mind

Is that the ultimate answer we chase after, hoping to find?

Life can be cruel. Life can be kind.

Life is not lived if it's lived resigned

EMPATHY

September 2018

How to speak about empathy without falling victim to visions of bleeding hearts decrying some injustice or other? Shocked? I am. For the simple reason that empathy is experience such a rapid decline in virtually every field of human endeavor, its failure alone could cause the end of the world. Oops. There it is. Just what I wanted to avoid. Yet, it is no less true.

Empathy for those of you who have seen the word but don't practice it regularly, it is the ability to share another being's experience indirectly, as if we could actually change place with them. If that doesn't seem all that important, then we have our work cut out for us.

From a purely cognitive point of view, empathy might be compared with the intellectual development of a child. Beginning as a unity, the child slowly emerges from this undifferentiated state by recognizing it's principal caregiver. A state of dependence reinforces this notion of there now being two entities – the subject, and this object, this person that relieves every state of discomfort, provides nourishment, and ensures the child's security. Over time, this differentiation expands to include others, be they living or inanimate.

What counts is the repeated exposure, the reliability of the encounter, and the significance of the interaction. Bit by bit, the world is constructed this way with objects that don't come and go as the child slips into periods of sleep between feeding, but acquire a permanence.

In these early stages, everything revolves around the child, its needs and physical sensations. Interactions with other children give rise to new experiences which will further expand the universe outside the child's self-awareness. And with this expansion comes conflict, from which will emerge the need to adapt and not just require. This ever enlarging experience of the outside world will ultimately bring about perhaps the single most significant factor in youngsters   of almost every species - the realization of the fundamental inadequacy of a purely subjective perspective.

Though we tend to employ the term only in relation to human interactions, it is clear that feels extend to all aspects of creation. Empathy transforms an idea into an experience, accompanied by physical sensations as a reaction to an event. Closely tied to our emotions, empathy offers the possibility to anticipate how others will respond, and to adapt our actions accordingly. It is the foundation of any successful individual or society in both present interactions, and in the projection of events into the future.

Too scientific an explanation? Perhaps you would have preferred a more prosaic, even poetic evocation. You will find that in the poem. But before reading it, before dismissing it as a nice to have part, but as current trends suggest, if indeed empathy is in decline, there is no question that our civilization with decline with it. That makes it perhaps quite a bit more difficult to dismiss.

Empathy is born of experience

When one was small and things made no sense

For reasons too numerous to explain

A spot spread into a stain

The root is there for all to see

Something in how others treated me

And how, in the mind of a child

I came to want the world to be mild

To live in a place where everything was alive

To see more the harmony than have to fight to survive

This place would function in accord with a set of rules

A general consensus clear enough even for fools

To look at a rock and sense its place as more than just fill

To look at an animal as more than something to hunt and kill

To see the oceans, churning with life

And think of something else than a gutting knife

The trees that were the lords of the land

Are they there waiting to be cut down, the entire stand?

To be turned into paper, or cardboard or wrap

Once used, to be burned or tossed into a hole, causing noa flap

Consumed in silence, what once was alive

Is that how we see the world? Only a place to survive?

A life is a life, it inhabits all things

If you listen closely, you can hear how Creation sings

Of course life and death form a perfect round

But each is accompanied by a different sound

At least for those who want to feel

Who see the cycle as a place to heal

Harm we must do, regret it we should

How else can in this world there ever be Good?

But what of the others, deaf to the noise

Creation's sounds and all of its joys

The waves that crash, the frogs that croak

The forest that comes alive when draped in night's cloak

The song of the whales, now garbled by sonar

The sweet silence in our heads drowned out by the car

The aimless chatter spoken into a cell

Who notices any longer the sound of the bell?

Or the birds that sing to welcome the day

I've known those immune, an annoyance they say

They soil our cars, spread disease, so chase them away

And those geese who live near our airports today

So what if we could have built them elsewhere?

So what if they've been there for millennia, we don't care

Were these souls born into the world already that way?

Can their eyes see no color other than grey?

Or did they suffer some deep hurt when young?

Into life too bruised, thoughtlessly flung?

Left to struggle against Life rather than alongside

Is that why from caring, from their hearts do they hide?

To care is a mixture of opposites strange

The result meant to lead to an embrace, not to derange

To stop, to hear, not run in some race

Passing too quickly through life leaving n'ary a trace

And what of those destined to come after we've left?

What did we leave them – a legacy to celebrate or a dump, bereft?

Has the distance between the present and future grown so small?

That hope is no longer part of the dance or the ball?

Always to want, though not knowing why

Can one pile one's possessions all the way up to the sky?

Would that suffice, could we still see to the top?

As we stand at the base with a pail and a mop

For to have means to take, there is no other way

And the mess that we leave by itself won't go away

A monument of marble once filled a hole

We wanted it so we took it, in fact, it we stole

Was any thought given to what we had done?

Or did all that matter was the side that won?

A general on a horse, raising high his sword

To stand there, a roost for pigeon shit, his reward

And the quarry, it had a history of its own

Rezoned, its story now by the wind blown

There is a choice:- to steward with care or exploit what was given

What's happened to that, by what from our minds was it driven?

I ask these questions with one goal in mind

Can we still imagine a world full of creatures, and to all still be kind?

DEVOLVING

October 2018

I began this poem not knowing where it would lead. But as I often do when a thought comes into my head, I write down the first line or two, and see what develops. I had recently shared a conversation with a friend to whom I tried to explain my perception of some fundamental differences that separate European and American cultures. This is always a slippery slope but if I miss that small window of opportunity to preface what I am about to say, rarely am I heard as intended.

In the 30 years spent in Europe, I began to understand that there are no shortcuts to a certain maturity. A heavy price is exacted, and one is not guaranteed survival or success. But since time marches only in one direction, it is always better to try and evolve in a positive direction. My point being that Europe has a long and bloody history filled with terrible crimes and mistakes. The last two world wars nearly destroyed Western European civilization. Yet from the rubble emerged a certain awareness that has lasted some 70 years, that there is more to gain by working together than by competing for imagined glory, superiority and dominance. The price is just too high.

Here in the States, we have less experience with tragedy than the centuries of European conflict. There is a certain youthful energy to this country that naturally is accompanied by a touch of arrogance characteristic of young Turks who have yet to taste the bitter wine.

It has been said that America is an idea, a set of human principles emanating from the Enlightenment. This was to be the land of liberty and freedom, where all were equal before the law, able to live as they pleased. It was a very tall order emanating from wealthy men for the most part who had the leisure to think big and far. Those occupying lesser stations in life would, it was hoped, rise up and approach the levels of the founders. As for the lapses and contradictions, the system was designed to allow for a certain degree of denial, to be determined on a case by case basis.

But it has also been said that the business of America is business, and nothing else. We are a secular country with one religion: Capitalism. Unfortunately, like most religions, the vast majority of practitioners have little idea what it actually is, and the form it exists under in our country. Paired with this boundless faith in ourselves – though periods of exception have existed – we came to define success not in the terms the founders would have approved of. But rather, success, as it is practiced in capitalism, is a quantitative endeavor, to be measured in terms of not what, but how much.

In a society where the basic needs are met and work is the normal observance of the capitalist religion, there was always assumed – though it turned out not to be true in all circumstances, even though it was considered dogma – that by working hard, one would succeed, i.e. make more money.

As often happens with young people, they get carried away by their enthusiasm, their desire to get started, and to get things done as quickly as possible. Two fundamental things are missing in this approach: first, the analysis rarely looks far enough into the future. Though the short term costs may be easy to identify, the longer terms ones offer suffer from a real neglect. The second, as long as someone else will pay the price, be it in the form of unwise loans or actually taking from some party lacking the strength to effectively defend itself, few raise any serious objections.

As I ventured into the conversation, I was careful to point out that my comments were of the observational, and not judgemental, sort. And that my goal was not to raise one example up and put the other down. Rather, what seemed to be to be an acceptable compromise, that we here are not, by definition, better, smarter, richer, stronger, wiser, more well loved than those from other nations. To entertain such a myth, as some politicians tend to do under the phrase "American Exceptionalism," is to create a myth that borders on fantasy, with only a tenuous relationship with reality. It creates unfulfillable expectations, accompanied by serious disappointment, which leads to resentment, social unrest and turmoil as those feeling let down have come to believe that nothing can be their fault, or if, on the odd chance that it might be, it is the responsibility – again unrealistic – for the government to come to the rescue.

In short, we have created a system based on misleading values, even some of which had so distanced themselves from those this nation was founded on. Without values – understood and embraced – there is neither sufficient direction nor purpose available to guide the collectivity. The nation's psychology begins to devolve, regress to a more primitive state where transactional, immediate motives drives what remains possible of its collective behavior. Instead of acquiring an ever more future oriented, inclusive perspective, one where the term "maturity," i.e. wisdom, would apply.

Nations, much like individuals, require time and purpose to pursue a positive development. And if there still remains enough maturity for us to recognize, the difference between those who have taken the proverbial high road to a more evolved station and those who have not, who have chosen the short term over the longer view, one might recognize a behavior more typical of an adolescent than a mature adult

This is not a scenario that promises long term success. So, if you find yourself having bought into the proverbial rat race (try visualizing that for a moment), chasing something you have come to realize you will never catch, it is not time to look for guilty parties elsewhere. We cannot change the system, nor should we necessarily want to do that. Make it work better, of course. But for that to happen, more of us have to think, learn, study, reflect, choose, AND VOTE.

In this age when people seem to believe that we can have it all, that an opportunity is a promise of success, there are too many flaws in that concept for me to even begin to examine here. Not to leave the matter open, when my first grandchild was born, I asked my daughter what kind of person did she hope to raise? Initially, the first terms that came to mind were healthy, happy, fulfilled – in short, successful. I then asked her what she meant by successful. Nowadays, the typical response would include money, position, security.. Nothing appears very wrong with that, though there was no mention of much beyond the child's immediate sphere.

But there is something wrong if we define success only by what affects our own individual interests. There is no question that we have the greatest chance of obtaining all those individual things if, in our values, we include the larger context. How much larger? As the world has shrunk, our vision needs to grow apace. Fall behind and we will fail to see the big picture. When that happens, those chances for success begin to decline apace as well. Something, in our "missing the forest for the trees" outlook, we have failed to pass on from parent to child. Unfortunately, a generation or two of parents have neglected a very significant part of what their children will now have to discover – and with much greater difficulty – on their own.

Our nation has developed a set of values based on the purely quantitative. It's about how much, not how worthwhile. It's very concrete, material, and very much anchored in the present moment. We tend to forget that what we do today will define what tomorrow looks like. So our decisions become more tactical. Though we employ the term strategy, I see very little of it around. The reason isn't that people have grown pessimistic of the future. It's that they define the future in terms of measurable things. Ironically, that approach limits their true value, for it something can be bought, how much can it really be worth. It's really only the things we can't buy that have lasting value.

The old saying about how we in the US "live to work," whereas in Europe, with a note of superiority, they "work to live." Rather a banal statement, yet full of meaning. The former suggests that value comes from the time and effort one devotes to establishing a situation. Insofar as all we have is time, spending it working means having less to devote to family, children, other more elevating endeavors. Of course we have financial obligations, but has money gone from being a means to an end, or has it simply become the end in itself?

A democracy requires more than just workers. It requires an informed, engaged, thoughtful electorate. If it was just workers, we would be less humanoid and more insectoid. Without dismissing the success of bee or ant colonies, with their clear definition of roles based on function, where individuals are born to execute that single function in the sole interest of the colony, I've not heard many people in favor of that model.

I've taken you on quite journey – as unexpected myself as you must be. Maybe we all needed a break from all that rhyming. It can get into one's head after awhile. So let me try and summarize:

This is not a critique of our system. It is a call for each one of us to devote some portion of their time to simply question what lies behind the choices they make. The first ones to come to mind will most likely be practical.   That's not really the answer.   Those are obligations resulting from choices. So you will have to back it up further. You don't necessarily have to go back to your early childhood, though ir might make the psychological community more prosperous. Go back to those values on which you base your decisions. Ask yourself how they came to be, where they came from, do they reflect what you truly believe. And consider then how well they have served you, what they cost you.

Should you discover that, in fact, they do not reflect what you truly think – if and when you take the time to think – then something is wrong. You have not been taking care of yourself, nor really living your own life. You have been living someone else's. If that's fine with you, if thinking about the one thing that is and will ever be truly your own isn't worth it, then you will have discovered a basic truth about yourself and about those who may, for whatever reason, share your perspective. But know just how much your are letting not just yourself, but everyone else, down.

There is that old expression about some people live to work while others work to live. The truth must lie somewhere in the middle, but only if there is balance. We all need a sense of purpose, of direction and that can be greatly enhanced by working. But if the recognition is inadequate, or worse, and if other options exist (and they always do, we just lack the vision to see them), to stay on that merry go round, the devolving door, will lead only to disappointment. Success is something we define, each one of us, insofar as it reflects our values, how we want to live, if consistency, consequence, honesty, integrity are among those we embrace.

Raise your children responsibly, knowingly, have learned to trust yourself by your own mistakes. If you need help, get it. But children are not accessories, they are not some part of an immature adult's life plan where each item is to be ticked off in a timely manner. Life is not a race nor a competition. It is a journey. It is your journey. Take it wisely, with curiosity to learn about the world and yourself. Pay the price maturity demands and the journey will be all the richer for it.. And your success, the inevitable success, will have become your own. Others will see it, many may admire it, because it has become who you are and no one can take that from you.

We used to call it pride in oneself. Now we call it self-esteem, and bemoan how in spite of all that material comfort and success, our children find themselves so lacking in it. Something is wrong, and every parent can fix it. You don't need a pill or a deep dive into your *childhood unless you need help. And there is no shame in asking for real help – not a crutch, but a different vision to guide you.*

If you feel you are on some merry-go-round, never forget that if you recall how you got on, you will know how to get off. Who needs more stuff   And if some huckster writes a book telling you to "lean in" or "you can have it all," they are lying. Even if we could have it all, what is "all" anyway? And why assume we would even want it? Where would we possibly put everything?

If the study of history comes to be spurned

If all of the knowledge that lives in our books is burned

The foundation of all that we know and have learned

Back to dark times will we be returned

For the past is the link to where we are now

It taught us to clear the land not with a hand but a plough

And from there we moved on, curiosity the fuel

Survival receded, civilization the tool

For time exists in three places at one time

The past, the present, and a future we hope will be fine

They are linked inextricably, foundation, walls and roof

How can anyone fail to see there is no other truth?

But something has changed, the truth has devolved

Instead of forward, they now have revolved

What might that mean for I know the word?

But never in this way has it ever been heard

Evolve suggests progress, a moving ahead

When failures were revealed, they were left for dead

Leaving their place to a higher form

So that these could then become the new norm

But devolve to me suggests another route

We go backwards, and progress becomes moot

Is this not as clear as money in the bank?

Or Is the writer just another crank?

Then try this image on for size

If it helps not at first, give it a few more tries

A revolving door, one that moves from left to right

Can spin with consistency all through the night

It turns in a fixed circle, providing a way in

How could that ever be taken for a sin?

Imagine now what might happen if for whatever reason

We continue to turn, not noticing the changing season

One more time we say, how could that hurt?

If we miss the exit again, will someone blurt

Though we push harder no exit we see

Something is wrong, and that something is me

When did a walk turn into a run

Though we talk about it often, we're having no fun

Have I missed more than just a way out

In chasing who knows what, have I forgotten what it's about

Where I began, and why did I choose

Did I think I could win, but never considered I could lose

We push harder hoping to accelerate the pace

Have we now turned a purposeful walk into a race?

But how do I stop, and once off what would I do?

Look for another one to get on, it's all that I knew

There are things more important than how much

Success can be defined by many things as such

The time missed with children, raised for pay

Business travel and time spent away

Moments that happen but once and never again

Were you there to see it way back when

Memories are the mortar by which a family endures

Making more money for later – empty lures

Run if you want, but close your eyes

You've missed what from the outside is easy to surmise

As life lived in blur, so our vision grows smalll

Lacking perspective, the obstacles grow tall

The end result, now trapped in a spin

Where's the way out and how did we get in?

Faster and faster we race as exhaustion prevails

No external wind can ever hope to reach our sails

Caught are we now, with no way out?

Is that what life has come to be all about?

WHEN YOU THINK OF ME, WHO DO YOU SEE?

October 2018

How often have you sensed an opening in a conversation with a friend where you might have taken it to a deeper level? Did you seize the occasion, or did you deem it "better" to let it pass by? Of course there are reasons society sanctions in the name of discretion: it's none of my business, they might misunderstand, I might inadvertently touch a raw nerve, we don't know each other that well, why risk the friendship, don't get involved. But have you ever considered that something might be lost?

The poem relates an ordinary incident while walking the dog with my Italian son-in law. He is a warm and openhearted individual who though most certainly loved by his family, never was exposed to the kind of understanding of himself and others that would provide a structure. I sense an interest, but not the practical means. And while talking, I realized the interrogation I was having with myself. I began to wonder how complete an image he might have of me. And in that moment, I realized I had a choice. I could keep our friendly relationship on a rather formal basis – son-in-law/father-in-law – or I could see if a deeper friendship might not be possible. Perhaps, might it not even be desired?

There have been occasions when our talks had slipped into a more personal territory – professional ambition – where he even mentioned that he had never had this kind of conversation with his own father who, by the way, is a warm and engaging man himself.

It seems that among men, there is a difficulty to establish closeness with their sons. The infamous "sex" conversation is one example, though it is more functional and information than personal in the sense of revealing the emotional dimension to sex. We tend to employ principally the convenient catchall term "love" as a sufficient foray into the world of men and their emotions.

And there it was. I had backed into a subject which I thought more than worthy, perhaps even necessary, to explore. Though easier for men to express their emotions with a woman, the lack of familiarity with the domain in general makes for a certain discomfort. That is a pity for emotions provide the personal substance of those values – mostly ignored on the conscious level, but always as operative in reality. Women seem to find it easier to employ their emotions in bonding with each other, while men resort (one might even say retreat) to more practical, concrete things.

What has been forgotten is the reason for friendship. The Greeks believed that friendship was a higher value than the concept of romance or love, which was the product of passion and desire. Friendship, they believed was not something readily available until a man had reached a certain maturity where the spiritual, the intellectual and the emotional could converge into something deeply meaningful.

This embrace of affection between men has been misinterpreted to suggest homosexuality, particularly as there are many literary references to physical affection being shared with younger men as well. It sheds perhaps more light on how we have come to view sex than how the Greeks themselves did. Were they perverse lechers, lusting after young men? Or were they perhaps a people who had understood that men need each other, as women need each other, to provide support and guidance on the road to realizing their gender identities?

I fear what we have lost is an understanding, an acceptance of caring, of expressing affection, without reducing it to a vulgar act devoid of any higher meaning.

The poem reflects a bit of this, in its conventional expression. It raises a number of questions: why do we even sense an opening if not to seize upon it? Does it really suggest a sexual component, or is sex not first and foremost an expression of vitality and attraction which has nothing to do with sex? Do things became physically sexual only when the higher expressions are blocked, the result of a frustrated need for closeness? Have we become afraid of our own emotions which by that very fact turns every healthy impulse into a base expression? Is it worth the risk? Why is it even a risk to be open and accept a certain closeness?

That's a lot of questions and I hope they give rise to even more as your read the poem. I don't offer answers. 'Questions are always so much more productive.

I was talking of late with my son in law

As we spoke, a question emerged, something new I saw

When we think of another, the closer the more true

Would it not be of interest to ask them what they knew?

Of ourselves, if the relationship is strong

Should we not have a clear idea as we continue along?

Without any awareness, a picture they possess

It lurks in the shadows, so they are left to guess

Who we are in our totality

So when they think of us they can clearly see

Who is this person in all their complexity

That conversation, unencumbered by confusion, may truly be

Why is it then only fragments exist?

Pieces of the puzzle while the essential is missed

When the whole person we are is misunderstood

And flawed assumptions do no one any good

Yet if that be the case the conversation offers little chance

For the subject discussed to really advance

Is it discretion? Is it fear?

Is that why we resist forming an image that's clear?

One that would open each one the other to understand

To be nourished unaltered, as we enter a new land

One where defenses have no need to exist

Where precious opportunities will no longer be missed

And preconceived notions, incomplete if not wrong

Linger no more, in this place where they do not belong

Or is it simply sloth, we're too lazy to think

Instead let's just go for something to eat and drink

To find our words grow ever more stale

And the reasons to share grow ever more pale

Perhaps it's both, there's a cocktail for sure

And a brew made for dissatisfaction to endure

It won't be spoken or even explicit

What we choose to hide is always illicit

Frustration creep, strained conversation

Has some new disease infected the nation?

Though at times, sneaking out from the past

Some matter of concern that you thought you'd cast

When the water looks clear and the fish swim

Give it a shot and jump in

If the opportunity is missed, felt by all

Up it goes one more floor, this alienation wall

Back into the shadows, an opening unresolved

It's done perhaps for good, the sin unabsolved

Banished the wish to share some confidence

Sent back to the shadows as if to do penance

But the secret that longed to be shared

Is left to perish as if no one cared

An uncomfortable silence, an opportunity gone by

Everyone felt it but no one dared try

Suddenly we're alone with the bill to pay

What's wrong with that person, to myself I might say

Interesting how my first thought is to blame

What frightens them so that they cannot name

And then I remember, I too could have spoken

Had I done so would something have been broken?

There is always a chance to speak one's mind

In the hope of some new complicity to find

Not everyone sees things as I do

In fact, I've found very few

Discretion they say is worth the price

Keep things social and the subjects nice

That will keep whatever we call this friendship on track

Had I spoken there might have been no way back

So there you have it, yet another choice

To what I see should I always give voice?

How many chances in the end do we get?

Is the risk worth the bet?

I might be wrong or I might be right

I want to live in the daytime, not some dark night

Many fall away, they don't understand

Sad it's becoming to live in this land.

For something is happening to which there's a cost

How many times have opportunities been lost?

There was a chance to connect and a chance to learn

Of the bridges Life offers, from how many away will we turn?

Who was this person I thought I knew?

We always got along, we were both part of the crew

Oh well, people are often like that

Alone with my questions, there I sat

SKULK OR SHOUT?

October 2018

The Reverend Martin Luther King once said something to the effect that one needn't worry about the extremes, for their numbers would never be overwhelming. It was rather those in the middle, those who were most numerous, but also the most inclined to remain silent, when their voices were needed the most.   Abstention, delegation, disengagement – all are sins which, in and of themselves, may not be of such great consequence. But when taken together, they constitute a wrong so significant, so far reaching that it brings with it a cost one chose not to acknowledge when it was still time.

I wrote this just before the mid-term elections, and following one of those many minor incidents one encounters frequently but more often than not, I was reminded of MLK's words. I found it disturbing that after 2 years of the current administration, so many people who feel they are of good conscience, prefer to avoid thinking, let alone speaking, about the challenges we are facing.

While I was away, living in Europe, there was a different tone given to the civil discourse at all levels of society. It was Switzerland, so one obviously cannot compare. But then, comparison is unavoidable if for no other reason than to provide perspective. Once again, it is observational, not judgemental, at least at this level of reflection.

Living in Europe, one gets a feeling of maturity, if not wisdom. The intellectual traditions are deeply rooted in the cultures, and bring with them a weightiness one does not find here. Class, authority, fear and a latent tension that has kept the dragon sleeping these past 80 years for the memory of the devastation is still close enough. Yet even the events of the last century are fading from memory, as the old demons are stirring again.

In the States, on the other hand, and though we never lived under the repressive yoke of the past as is the case in Europe, we have waged a war on formality which has brought us a casualness bordering on the dismissive. Perhaps it was necessary when it began because our insularity, our provincialism preceding the great wars, had held us back. And our role during those wars, our success, and the exaggerated myths we created about ourselves fostered an equally exaggerated sense of confidence in our righteousness and our cultural, political, scientific and economic superiority.

But ours was of the pragmatic sort, born in the present, not the past, and pointing clearly at the future. As with the war on formality, there was little thought given to the consequences of our penchant for abandoning anything older that a few years. With it we have witnessed a cultural epidemic of ADHD, now medicalized, so conveniently taken out of our hands and placed in those of doctors and the pharmaceutical industry. And those individuals suffering from PTSD are now as much a part of yet another epidemic which has also become medicalized, thereby further removing any responsibility.

Not that long ago, we spoke in terms more spiritual than biological. Terms such as alienation, a sickness of the soul, the search for meaning were more current. Their usefulness resided in the fact that they offered a way forward in dealing with symptoms of depression, disaffection, loneliness, and the growing challenge of material wellbeing – as ironic as that may be. When we have to struggle simply to survive, we need each other and find the means to subsume our differences to the exigencies of reality. But remove these pressures, our differences, often a byproduct of the competitive capitalist model, emerge. We see others as a means to an end for our own advancement and not as the key to our collective survival.

This avenue is seen as a challenging one for even though it offers a way forward, it requires considerable effort and introspection. With all the distractions offered today, there is little time, and less interest, in investing that time in the only thing we truly possess – ourselves.

And true to the American pragmatic, binary approach to things, the solution we found was to take social and psychological challenges that are quite normal in life has been to simply medicalize them. Instead of there being a sickness of the soul, a spiritual void – spiritual simply means transcending ourselves - we now have an epidemic of psychiatric ailments, quickly diagnosed almost mechanically, and accompanied by a pharmaceutical remedy.

No longer must we struggle with ourselves, to know ourselves, and thereby empower ourselves to own and direct our lives. We are sick, we go the doctor who claims – directly or otherwise – to have the means to cure us. And the cure? Pills. And the consequence? A constant progression of psychological malaise, an aimless population whose only goal is to enrich themselves materially, rising rates of suicide and anxiety conditions, and an epidemic of addictive medications that were supposed to treat, if not cure, us.

From this perspective, we have made the problem far worse. By reducing the sense of ownership of oneself, by making issues of adaptation to life's normal challenges into a medical condition for which the individual no longer has the means to ameliorate themselves, we have produced a culture of patients.

For those who were anticipating a pleasant moment of reverie in rhyme, I must apologize. Though I may use the form, its purpose is clear. And by having the ability to slip through the normal defenses of pure rationality, perhaps the message will find a home. For I fear that if we continue much further down this path, we will no longer know how to do what Nature designed us to do – to experience, to learn, to discover our own inner resources, and ultimately to survive.

I am speaking out in what is, I hope, a substantive and substantiated manner to provoke a new thoughtfulness, a reflection that goes deeper than the obvious, and targets the way we address our challenges so that we actually take the time to understand the origins and true nature of whatever affliction we may be called up to address rather than rushing past everything we might have known from the past, to find and, of course, claim the credit for some new miracle medical discovery.

Our bravado, our "exceptionalism," and our (what's the opposite of deepening?) superficiality in eschewing anything that is not biological, our incipient anti-intellectualism, and our rejection of a liberal education in favor of a vocational training point in the direction of recreating a new "worker: - not "working" – class that has abandoned the means of its own potential progress.

I am not as pessimistic as I may sound, for by nature I am rather a cheerful person. But I have seen too many instances of people – young people with potential and a future – abandoning the means they posses to build their lives as an expression of their individuality to the benefit of all. Through drugs, compulsive, even abusive, sexual practices, anxiety and suicide, we are being warned by Nature itself. Yet for many reasons discussed in these poems, we have gotten lost in a world of external distractions and don't seem to know how to find our way back.

There is a good place to complete the circle. We all have a personal stake in the proper functioning of our society. As numerous and as diverse as we are, achieving a level of civility and mutual tolerance is no small matter. But unless we speak out thoughtfully, substantively and respectfully when we encounter a wrongful act or statement, the perpetrators feel validated, the victims feel abandoned, and those in the middle withdraw even further.

If this is the path we are on, then our chances for that long run we all hope for fall seriously into question. That we can solve practical problems is certain. What might be lacking, however, is the awareness of our shared destiny. If we lose that, there remain only the centripetal forces, already in evidence, waiting to tear us apart. And if that happens, what shall become of us?

Here is a question worth thinking about

When you see an egregious wrong, do you skulk or shout?

Do you approach the person with fire in your eye?

And an indignant soul that such wrongs it you won't buy

Or is your approach more diplomatic in style?

To reason and convince and consider for awhile

What they have done, why and what were they thinking

Or did they stand watching, without blinking?

To start, on our concept of right and wrong, let's reflect

Who nowadays sets aside busyness, making it hard to detect?

Where once the rules were clear, and we used to know

Carelessly abandoned, they now have become less so

Leaving the impression they no longer apply

We've even forgotten how to ask why

Is that even possible, that they no longer exist?

Or in our educational system, have we something was missed?

If that be the case, with who lies the blame?

Is there one person or too many to name?

Should we be worried, are right and wrong notions out of date

We find refuge in nuance and equivocate

Splitting hairs until nothing remains but grays

If that be the case truly numbered are our days

How to decide which way to turn?

With no right or wrong, how does one learn?

Repressive, authoritarian, rigid and unfair

Some believe this, as into some oblivion they stare

Is everything now reduced to an individual transaction?

The only measure of its value being my personal satisfaction

Each one serving a different and changing vision

How long before erupts a cosmic collision?

The other is no longer neighbor or friend

The fabric is torn in a way that we cannot mend

Its progress has been slo, but steady and sure

As each one's perspective shrank, its only mission to endure

Competition drives the process of our lives

But instead of justice will remain only the knives

Without the glue civilization provides

It will cease to exist if no one abides

And what we now have, taken for granted

Will erode until little remains of the seeds we have planted

Warnings abound, solutions unclear

What we are doing, no one wants to hear

We turn away, the future is still so far away

What counts is only what happens today

Is that true? Is the future bleak

Or is it ourselves who have grown selfish and weak?

No purpose other than to gratify

And have enough money so all we want we can buy

Can a society exist with no direction worthwhile

If right and wrong are gone, on what base can we smile?

Do we just wait, stuck in some present tense?

Until it comes to an inevitable end, we maintain the pretense

We've taken a brief tour, it seems to me clear

The only motivation that works now is imminent fear

Each minor wrong when combined every day

Weakens those pillars as we chip away

What of the right? I've spoken of only one side

Do we know what that means any more or has it died?

Is it old fashioned to believe, have they all lied?

Has history departed leaving only some random wave to ride?

I think not, there I've said it out loud

We need some reason of ourselves to be proud

Neither to boast nor rewards to claim

But to know our vision clearly so its values we can name

If they need revision, let's have that talk

In my book it's always wrong just to walk

Does saying it necessarily make it so?

Clearly not, but I can tell you why if you care to know

Be it ignorance, selfishness, green or sloth

Our current approach is stretching to its limits the cloth

Small tears appear, so far it can hold

Now may be your last chance to step up and be bold

So next time you see something you feel is wrong

Something in our world that does not belong

Pause for a moment and look deep inside

Will you speak up or by your silence will you join the wrong side?

PERFECTION

October 2018

I have written extensively about my years abroad, how I changed, but also how in the one and a half generations which came during my absence, this country has changed. The poem is a rough sketch, a caricature, not intended to represent any one individual, but a generational average. As often happens, we tend to focus on the more privileged as their examples are often more extreme. And exaggeration is a useful tool to illustrate something no one really wants to examine in a sincere and constructive way.

In reading what follows, and the poem itself, try and experience it as a complaint, in the classic sense, and not complaining. I worry about these young people for too many of them are lost, burdened with a desperate need for approval, yet a terrible fear of being hurt. Their difficulties in establishing honest, committed relationships flow from how they were raised – as perfect reflections of their parents unrealized dreams and adolescent aspirations. This has left them with an identity so far from their inner selves that the slightest remark can shake their entire edifice. Everything they feel they are resides on the surface. They need to look, but not necessarily be, perfect. And in the absence of perfection, anything less than a "8" constitutes a social death sentence.

We have led a generation to productize itself. That is a cruel bequest to leave and one those who enabled it have a responsibility to try and correct it But how when, for the most part, the harm is done? And how many parents, fragile themselves in their patched together self-images, can face their gravest mistakes.

We've called our culture one of Narcissism in the belief that to be narcissistic is to be in love with oneself, and one's external image. This is a derivative definition, since narcissism is a developmental issue. Narcissists are not in love with themselves insofar as they have feelings for themselves. Rather, these are people whose emotional development has been incomplete. They are stuck in some adolescent loop with behavior reminiscent of teenagers – enamored of themselves in a very superficial, egocentric way. Incapable of seeing things as yet from any perspective other than their own, their perception of reality is fragile and flawed. And they lack the means to address, in a more mature, more complete manner.

These are not happy people for though they may put on a show to convince others, what they are truly doing is trying to convince themselves that the image they have created is themselves. It I not, for had it been so, they would be equipped to face the challenges of life without clinging to some idea of their own perfection when children, but which, for reasons unclear, no longer applies Stripped of their imaginary armor, they see their own vulnerability.

Rather than face it, understand why it is so and what they can do about it, they double down on their efforts to hold this fragile persona together. In the most severe circumstances, living can become too hard. If all else fails, if their efforts to adapt express themselves as an external adaptation that may look adequate, designed to fool others – themselves generally as superficial and self-absorbed - the direst of outcomes emerges as possible.

The central issue is that the parents may be more mature than their offspring, but got lost in their own narcissistic fantasy, rendering themselves dependent on it. And when a child develops a serious problem – drugs, sex, criminality, health – and needs its parents firmly grounded in reality, many parents are incapable of seeing the error of their own ways, and focus on counterproductive approaches based on "what is wrong with my child: When in fact, the child, though suffering, may be far more mature than the parents on whom they can only superficially rely. If pressed, they may invoke that age old distum: 'If I ever have to choose between myself and us, I will always choose me."

At this point, they child, having no recourse to air its grievances and redress he situation can only acquiesce in silence, since the parents will refuse to acknowledge the child's point of view. What kind of options remain? Drug addiction, anxiety disorders, sex, criminality – all a cry for help. But if the price of help is too high for those who must provide it, the child will be – in whatever form possible – sacrificed to "save' the rest of the family.

Which brings me to the central question:

We often make fun of Millenials, their cluelessness, their disengagement, their fear of commitment, and their general "all about me" outlook, as if it was their fault. I would posit that if it is a responsible party we are looking for, we would be better served by going back one generation. But this is not about assigning blame, just understanding how a generational mindset came to be. Not that the Millenials are a lost generation or need fixing through some massive social intervention. All they need is some honest parenting, an example set by those who claim to be adults but who act, themselves, more like teenagers.

These pseudo adults too often act as if they were the children in some national toy store where everyday should be Christmas. There is a general absence of character, defined as the ability to defer gratification without suffering a serious bout of resentment or worse. Character is not based on a simple act of will because someone decided one day it was so. Character is based on the ability to see beyond oneself, where others are as much a part of the equation as oneself. It is something one develops over time, built on experience as one questions, refines and ultimately embraces a set of values which will guide us through our lives.

Without character, there can be no consistence, no sense of consequence or responsibility. And without that, can any complex society hope to address its challenges, find the will to overcome differences, and the courage to do what is required for the greater good?

That's quite a bit to put on a few lines that rhyme. But I have found these issues so lacking in our rush towards money, success, celebrity, influence, and many of the other purely external criteria too many base their lives on. We have forgotten somewhere along the way that the rugged individual we like to compare ourselves to is a thinking individual, a caring individual, a responsible individual who does not depend on others, but who can ask for help when needed all the while striving for their own independence, and will gladly return the favor whenever needed. Put in this way, it should become obvious what we need to continue this grand experiment of our in the hope of a successful outcome, and what is so seriously missing in our discourse and behavior now.

Without character, on the individual level, there can be no character on the national level either. In its absence, everything else becomes so much harder as to be viewed by too many, as impossible.

Some grow up under their parent's protection

Safe and secure, every need provided before its detection

They learn to want things they will never need

Every wish every cry every desire their parents heed

Doe s anyone realize what these children of plenty learn?

Other than in life one must always to yearn

For something new, something with flash

Who needs a job or independence as long as there's cash?

And while this goes on, the example set by Mom and Dad

Who think they are helping by offering all they never had

The kids were happy when this all began

But now they don't seem to enjoy all the glam

A teacher might make a comment one day

Your child's attention wanders, should this continue he won't be able to stay

Did I I forget to mention they are in a private school

To stay in the public system would have been too cruel

So tutors are hired, coaches as well

We're not raising a child but a product to sell

We spoke to the headmaster, the teacher doesn't understand

With our progeny one must use a knowing and deft hand

We pay all this money, so the grades must reflect

Just how perfect our kids are, with no flaws to detect

Somehow the grades improve, they are college bound

Equipped with a self-esteem that won't touch the ground

Things change there, they no longer come easy

Never having learned how to work makes the stomach queasy

Pills for this, drugs for that, anxious not knowing what to do about that

I saw this cool guy before, he wore thisincredible hat

I've got to have the very same one

If I don't how will I ever have any fun?

Should I run to the mall or can it wait

I don't have the money so the parent must bait

Graduation comes, they've made it through

You've had to help if there was to be a laureate shiny and new

Now for the job, who do we know?

Set it all up, get them ready and dressed for the show

Thank goodness they learned how to deliver the talk

Fools them every time so he never has to walk

Nailed the interview with skill, the job is well done

Let's do something different, after that interview they'll need fun

"Here you go honey, how could they not see?

Just what a prize you are and will always be"

The child smile warmly, though it's a fake

All they did was smile and be charming – is that all life will take?

Monday comes, for the train they will wait

Bummer, they are all tired, last night finished late

This job thing, is this really my, is it meant for me?

Maybe take a year off go through Europe – parents will pay, so for me it'll be free

They give me a desk, is this a joke?

And the pay? I might as well be broke

The stuff they give me any idiot could do

Can't they tell I'm perfect? I thought they knew

Day after day, the same old grind

Is this what my folks really had in mind?

I'm better than this, that's what everyone used to say

What's wrong with these people, I wish they would all go away

I tell the parents this isn't working out

It's not at all what I want or what I'm about

But something is wrong, for the very first time

They start telling me I need to get into line

When did this happen? Was it all a lie?

Somebody please, the anxiety, tell me why

It's all rather simple, you were raised to believe

It wasn't exactly a lie, though they did deceive

It was easier to give you things, the pressure of parenting
to relieve

They got the new gospel, and the new grace they did
receive

Everyone, they said, now could have it all

All you need do is believe and stand tall

Be noticed for the product you've now become

In the world of your mind ,you will always be number one

Sadly there is a lie you were told

It's a big one, and it doesn't seem to grow old

You were the best, self-esteem came first

No matter reality, though you might be the worst

You saw how the system could be played, money rules

Working hard to prove oneself, that's just for poor fools

So there it is, the truth finally arrives

As long as the surface meets expectations, the system thrives

Until some substance is required, style can no longer suffice

And all of that greatness turns to ice

What to do now, parents are no longer rich

They've stopped buying me somethingeach time I have an itch

Dad lost his job, Mom is displeased

Our lives now suck, almost diseased

Here's my dilemma, at least that I see

There's not much that I know that's inside of me

I relied on the praise that was never earned

No one told me about the bridges I'd burned

Full speed ahead, every door opens wide

Now that I know the truth, I just want to hide

My confidence crumbled like a castle built on sand

But my friends, maybe they'll understand?

With things changed and not working as before

Some have cut me off, some have closed the door

I guess that's how things get fixed, like it or not

Something went wrong and started to rot

I don't know if I have it in me to start over again

They taught me to talk, so maybe I'll take up a pen

And write about the only thing that I know something about

Me – maybe I'll be famous and rich after all – fuck doubt!

TO GO WIDE OR GO DEEP

January 2019

I was reflecting on current trends in selecting one's partner, and how they have changed over the past twenty to thirty years – possibly more. There was a time, longer ago than that, that marriages were in one way or another arranged. Women were entirely dependent on men for their place in society and for their material well-being. Pregnancy before marraged has always existed, but in stricter times, it was a principal concern. And men may have thought they could dabble, but often had to pay for the privilege. Nowhere in this scenario was there much talk of romance or love. It was simply assumed that if one had a chosen partner, love would come in time.

With the newfound financial freedom from which women now benefit, the traditional roles have grown less imperative, leaving a much greater leeway for experimentation, but also for confusion. Like it or not, we are heavily influenced by the expectations of our social environment. And with these changes, beginning in the sixties, came all sorts of variations. With no guidelines, no precedents existing or desired, anything was possible..

Due to the lack of an y set parameters, measurement of success could only be empirical. In terms of determining the acceptability of any given model, there were civil records of marriages, births, divorces, and deaths. There is one more thing we could measure, but which we probably don't know how to do it, i.e. the longevity of the model.

The consequences of these changes should have been easy to predict, but if they were, little to no serious debate occurred. Men felt license to sleep with as many women as he could, since the fear of unwanted pregnancy had been reduced to close to nothing. And selfish, rather immature creatures that we are – in the absence of responsibilities – "going wide" has in general been widely embraced. The impact here was a growing fear of entrapment – possibly more imagined than real. Some have speculated that such a fear was natural for men given their evolutionary role to populate. Examples obviously exist in the animal kingdom.   However, as we have been living in one form of society for hundreds of thousands of years, it is equally reasonable to dismiss that explanation as vestigial.

It is no great stretch to go from fear of entrapment to avoidance of trust, and from there, to a fear of intimacy. Just how real and justified are these fears? I leave it to you to ponder the question. What I can say is that on the male side of the equation, the objectification of the male ideal as defined by external rather than internal values, young men's insecurities and uncertainties have increased.   Other sources of uncertainty come from the new roles women have assumed along with their expectations of a gentler man.   And finally, the AIDS/STD epidemics, though they accompanied an increased promiscuity, have ironically erected new barriers to intimacy.

Without the means to validate themselves as men, through the adoption of certain roles in society – these roles no longer being as widely embraced, there remains the easiest, most elemental form of expressing masculinity , i.e. sex – though in this case, with no redeeming social value.

Women, though have acquired a well deserved freedom and independence, though they not surprisingly don't always know what to do with it. For they too have seen the traditional roles, confining as they were, dissolves, leaving little certainty in their roles. Whereas women were objectified in other times, they – like men – have become productized. Whereas previously they were the ones being chosen with little to say about it, they are now in a position to do the choosing too.

But with choice comes uncertainty, as too many options reduce the likelihood of knowing how to make a sound selection.

So, women now find themselves in the unenviably similar situation as men, l;e. with responsibilities they don't always know how to assume. More and more confusion on all sides. Though there is much debate and as many opinions, there is little consensus on a societal way forward. To simply promote individual choice bodes ill for society which requires more coherence than "do whatever you want" can provide.

Romance, in the traditional sense, has lost much of its place, now taken over by this culture of transaction. Here too, the consumerism becomes evident as women will use untested criteria to select a man, often knowing mostly what he is, not who he is. The problem here is further complicated by that fact that the interest in knowing who we are has waned, as individuals have come to embrace the much easier to demonstrate "what" and not the "who."

When neither gender finds a social complementarity beyond sex, everyone is deprved of the means to learn about trust in a more relaxed, natural, less commercial environment. The result, I fear, is a trend towards disconnection, as characterized by this mania to stay connected technologically constantly.

Aml not so subtly promoting the "deep" approach? Caught. But there are reasons, and I believe, important psychological reasons for this. First, we cannot live in this world without having learned to build trusting relationships – romantic or otherwise. That requires time, *effort and a personal investment in terms of learning to know someone else, with the added benefit of learning to know oneself at the same time. The sexual encounter in the true sense, and not the "doggie-style fucking" which has gained considerable ground on the field of sexual engagement, is based on one person physically penetrating another. Both are vulnerable, and are keenly aware of everything that is at stake. Confidence is easy to feign, but in its true absence, and though one may simulate pleasure, such facsimiles lend themselves to the development of serious long term consequences. Ultimately, engaging one person rather than many presents many psychological challenges which each individual will benefit from if they are met.*

Second, focusing on one privileged relationship leads to the creation of bonds of friendship and the discovery of the fundamental values of loyalty, trust, honesty, integrity – all essential in the development of character. These are values which not only support the couple, but the family, the community and the nation at large. Without them, large groups will always ultimately sink back n conflict and chaos.

And Finally, perhaps most importantly, dedicating oneself to one long term goal brings purpose, direction, meaning and a confidence in oneself and another, which are, in fact, the rewards we value more and more as we get older. To willfully embrace a "superficial" lifestyle deprives the individual, society and indeed civilization of those things which provide significance.

This is not a moral judgement, but a psychological one. Open relationships, having someone on the side, cheating – all are viable models in the present to near term. And one can certainly justify them, for even in the best of circumstances, monogamy is a considerable challenge. In some viable form, it alone can breed trust and lasting, meaningful bonds. And it can improve a physical relationship because with confidence and trust, curiosity and a sense f adventure grow, all necessary if the sentiment of vulnerability is to be overcome.

To live widely is to ultimately live alone. We remain a stranger all our lives. It is just a fact. That doesn't mean that one should remain in a bad relationship, insofar as one has done one's best to achieve something. Life is about building, and that includes relationships. To go from one to the next, intent on avoiding any commitments, may have made sense when our species were not numerous and were themselves constantly living under threatening circumstances. We don't have to worry so much about that nowadays. But ask yourself this:

Is each new encounter, perhaps exciting before it happens, ultimately disappointing once it has taken place? Not every partner will inspire, and may in fact cause one to retreat back into oneself, just doing the minimum of what needs to be done. Routine replaces discovery,. And there is the matter of constantly searching for the next partner. Desire gives way to "horneyness," itself seriously misunderstood as having a high sexual drive that is "hard-wired" into our "brain." To see things this way is to reduce oneself to a set of rather primitive, instinctive drives to which we are only slaves enrolled in its service. That might shock some of you, but in fact, that's what's happening.

Sex has a higher potential than just a quick, sweaty orgasm. It is a language, a conversation, a means for two individuals to literally join physically and emotionally. To anyone who has ever made love, there can be no doubt of its impact, lasting benefit, and unique role in further establishing one's own significance.

I wrote a poem awhile ago entitled "Somebody, Anybody, Nobody. The point being to track the evolution – or rather the devolution – from significance to insignificance, to inexistence.

Fun , a word which exists as its own noun, does not exist in that many languages – though it does in ours. Other words are used to convey a similar meaning, but rarely can one find a precise translation.. Though an essential part of life, it could never be its principal objective.

So, please excuse the football metaphor, but somehow it felt right.

Go wide or go deep

Go flat or go steep

That will determine what you keep

For those who go wide, it's a numbers game

Who matters little for they all are the same

Can you even remember if it was wild or tame

Some say the reason is the fear of intimacy

To experience requires a fair dose of vulnerability

So stay on the surface and nothing see

One after another, do you keep a list

Of who you did and whether you kissed

The night was passionate, in the morning dismissed

Oh, they weren't so great after all

Did you manage any connection to forestall

It's like going home, yet living in the hall

Can you sense how your loneliness grows

Or is it just a vague malaise that everyone knows

Can you still just dismiss it for fear of getting lost in its throes

While one it was easy and you were young

The music you listened to everyone sung

Did we even kiss, was there any tongue?

It sure did feel get to get rid of those rocks

Reminds he when I was just like all the other jocks

Who thought not with their brains, but with their cocks

Now that you're older, I can't help wondering

Did those too many partners anything of value bring

Were there any new melodies or lyrics to sing

Or was it always the same old tune

That when you were 30 you could still croon

Come to think of it – do you still moon?

You're middle aged now, still time to play

All those judgey people and their nay say

If you did something wrong, of course the price you'll pay

When once you believed it, you could laugh it off

Now when you try too hard, you only cough

And have you noticed, there's not much left in the trough

So here you are, alone at last

Life sure has been a never ending blast

And boy did it sure fly by too fast

Thinking back, there sure were good times

But the names and the faces – nothing rhymes

What was it after all that so fueled you many crimes?

It's never too late to take stock

A full review, once around the block

You can't open the door though there is no lock

It's your mind that's sealed shut, don't you see

You've been chasing your own tail, wanting only to be free

And the cherished freedom has left you lonely

What will remain of your time here once your days are spent

And you realized you never owned your life, you only rent'

From a house to an apartment, and finally a tent

Have you learned anything that you could pass along

To the group of those who made bad choices belong

And skimmed through life with a smile and a song

How long will the echo of your presence last

If your life went by quickly, what else will go fast

And as you time grows shorter, was it really such a blast?

On now to those who put down stakes

With gardens and leaves and flowers and rakes

Who found "the one" who loves to make cakes

It's true at the time you didn't know why

You picked this one over the one that was shy

Remember the secret shrug that came with "let's just give it a try"

The early years were great, always busy having fun

Building a career and going for a run

And there was the dream of your golden years lying in the sun

But that's for later, time now for the kids

Was it more than you bargained for, though it was you who put in the bids

If only children came with tight fitting lids

The years they flew by, there were moments of joy

Did you spend enough real time with your girl and your boy

Or did you seek refuge from the hubbub with some
technological toy

Raising children is a challenge unsuspected

Each partner has an agenda that remains undetected

And the struggle for supremacy does not respect any elected

Each decision is preceded by a serious discussion

Will the children be raised Catholic or Orthodox Russian?

And does our boy really want to play percussion?

That little girl has grown, no longer a princess

She's slovenly, self-absorbed and you're in distress

For she say she's not going to school – life's such a mess

A few snapshots to hopefully make you smile

This has gone on for quite awhile

But if you've read me before you know it's my style

Now back to you, if you saw your choice through

It was a purpose a mission, something you just knew

Did you read some book or were you given a cue?

And that adorable woman you married and made your wife

There were more than a few days when you'd have put her to
the knife

To swallow your anger and pride, ah the joys of married life

But joys there are – secure and stable

And more often than not there is something on the table

After dinner, just the two watching a movie on cable

No more need to forage for someone to do

Those bars you use to frequent, there remain but a few

And those poor souls on the internet, what a motley crew

IGNORANCE

October 2018

This Is a subject which has increasingly imposed itself on me since my return. It was something of an awakening for me when I went to live in Europe. Growing up in New York, the authenticity of Brooklyn and its neighborhoods conveyed a sense of sophistication and worldliness that was seriously inflated. Once I left for school upstate, I realized that the only people I had known were others quite like myself ethnically speaking. The outliars were those who were somehow marginally different. But to the rest of us, they seemed almost foreign. Suddenly I/ was in touch with people from the Midwest. My prejudice was to be gracious but secretly culturally superior, given my origins. But that too was quickly dispelled as it became obvious that other people may not have everything available to them, but since we weren't season ticket holders to anything, our culture was passed along more by osmosis than by any real acquaintance.

Going away to school was a very challenging, but ultimately very positive experience. The four years I spent in undergraduate study at an excellent small liberal arts college with a strong emphasis on sports as well, began a process of expansion that had been more pretension than reality. I was introduced to the world of ideas that I did not suspect existed. Though not intellectuals, my parents were intelligent, interested in the world, and traveled extensively. And when I declared my intention not to follow the normal path from History major to Law School, but rather to go to Switzerland to study clinical psychology, they never wavered in their support.

I never knew what they actually felt. My mother used to bemoan the fact that children, instead of living within walking distance of their parents, now straddled the world. Though not all of us did. My sister, three years my senior, had far more limited ambitions – though she graduate Phi Beta Kappa at her elite women's college. Her goals were to be engaged by her junior year, and married within a few weeks after graduation. Professionally, and in spite of her credentials, though I'm not so sure about her capabilities, she never wavered from wanting to become a teacher. There is no question that she followed very narrowly prescribed path most girls of her generation embraced without a second thought.

I wasn't aware of my own intellectual curiosity having more or less coasted successfully through school I hadn't been taught about hard work, ambition, drive – things just came to me. However fortunate that may appear, I believe the sooner we learn about those things, thebetter off we are. But my parents, and my father in particular, saw no role for himself in me becoming a man. All I knew was what I had been told – don't even think about having my own business, for that was what my father did. I was told I would have a profession. There was never any question. But which one? Colgate University, at the time, was known for its Philosophy and Religion department. I had a vague notion as a 17 year old – still a boy, not yet a man – of what the word meant. But what it really meant, the study of knowledge, was an entirely new concept. And as part of our imposed curriculum, I had to take several philosophy courses I found them intellectually challenging for their rigor, their process, and the underlying desire to understand that which we can only grasp but never possess.

I had two courses in particular – one on Ethics, and another on Depth Psychology and Religion – which marked me The first I took during my freshman year, and found the dialectic the small classes and the annoyingly open-mindedness of the professor, frankly refreshing. For perhaps the first time in my life, I was challenged to think deeply, to analyze, and then develop a substantiated point of view. I was 17, so I'm not very sure just how embarrassed I might be if I were to read it today. But it awoke in me the seeds of a confidence, an awareness, that had laid dormant throughout my public school years.

The second course, which I took in my senior year, was known to be very challenging and was difficult to gain acceptance to. The professor was a wry older man of Scandinavian descent, who took great pleasure in flummoxing us with readings from Kierkegaard, Hegel, and many others.   Their use of language was so refined, so intentionally convoluted, that it was a struggle. But it was at that moment that I realized my own native curiosity, my desire to understand, and the need for me to break free from the path I was on.

Simultaneously, there was an emotional awakening and probably my first real experience of love – or what we are capable at 20 years of age. Through a curious intersection of events and encounters, I met a girl who – I only learned later that she was engaged to someone else at the same university – a secret she kept from me for many months as she alternated weekend visits between her fiancé and myself. Initially, she was perhaps flattered by the attention someone more sophisticated seeming than either herself or her fiancé, might be interested. I was smitten by her country naturalness. And before either of us realized it, she was smitten as well. There is no question – love is blind – as it was always intended to be.

Love disrupts in that we are quite often attracted to someone who appears complementary to ourselves. However, the complementarity escapes completely our consciousness. It comes from the unconscious with a singular purpose – to point us in the direction of discovering the totality of ourselves. It is only with some external challenge that we drawn into a journey that can last a lifetime. It is the road back to ourselves.

Suddenly everything seemed possible. Another coincidence allowed me to spend a month in Switzerland where doors kept opening without hardly any effort on my part. And before I knew it, the LSATs I had taken, the applications to law schools I had submitted- all were forgotten. I was off to Switzerland to study something I knew very little about. Though I'd taken a psychology class at Colgate, I found it singularly uninspired, and did poorly. It was the American penchant forreductionism, binary thinking, the mechanization, /operationalization and medicaliztion of ourselves.

The personal digression figures has its place here because hopefully, it shows how certain aspects of a real education – and not just training, which is obviously essential as well – can open a mind convinced it know it all already or worse, doesn't need to know more. And it can entirely change the course of a life. Few things can do that.I told my own children to take advantage of these four years. They are the only time in our lives when we can devote ourselves to growing our minds. That's something that forms the basis for all the rest.My exposure to different ways of thinking – personally, culturally, professionally – and the realization that each culture believes it possesses the truth, even if the basic assumptions are fundamentally different. They are and they should be for the truth is composed of many facets, and we can never complete the picture using only our own perspective. To understand this requires extensive personal exposure, the desire to open one's mind rather than close it, secure in the limited knowledge we have, pretending it is far more authoritative than it is.

The size of a research budget does not determine what size piece of the "truth" pie on gets.

Facts come and go over time as our understanding grows. And that understanding should be an uninterrupted process, a movement forward. It should not be inspired by gain or prestige. Philosophy – the love of knowledge, or wisdom (even better). The former can be accumulated. The latter can only be earned, which is what makes it so precious.

Ignorance, on the other hand, is the enemy of progress, a dark force that seeks to annihilate rather than nurture. We had created an educational miracle in the country, first with our public sch l system, next with our universities, and currently our graduate schools and research institutions. The need was recognized from the beginning by the founders, for the intellectuals behind the Enlightenment, itself behind the notion of self-government, and ultimately democracy, knew that for it to have any chance of success, it required an informed and concerned electorate.

There was always an elitist strain running through the private schools. But the success of the public school system opened the doors to success by offering a quality education to those who could little afford one. Everyone benefitted.

Unfortunately, during the sixties, we began a necessary, but ill inspired tinkering with public schools which had too often intentionally sought to exclude segments of the population, depriving them of opportunity. There was an objective in mind – ensuring that they remained a permanent underclass.   There followed several decades of huge expenditures, tremendous disruption, a mass exodus of those who

could afford it from the public system, leading to a concentration of the very groups for whom integration was desired. The road to hell…..

Now, someone supposedly as progressive and pro-education as President Obama, is seeking to reduce the availability of a liberal arts education in favor of vocational training. I find this shocking as it is the antithesis not only to his own personal story, but contrary to the needs of our society.   For since the sixties, the quality of our more classically inspired educational model has suffered in favor of more cultural relevance. The result has been greater per student expenditures that virtually any other country, accompanied by declining scores across the board.

We have created several generations of vocationally trained, yet classically ignorant individuals who did not benefit from the expansive and rigorous exposure that can come only from a liberal arts education.

What is achieved by vocational training on a massive scale, as a doomed strategy to prepare a workforce commensurate with the needs of industry. Of course we need to ensure employment is available. But what happens to society when people are trained in marketing or *accounting but know nothing of philosophy or literature? Study programming and what will we have? People who know how to program and create video games or other sources of distraction that have already won the war against reading.*

One need look no further than the 2016 election to understand the gravity of our failure to educate ourselves. Should we not discover the errors of our ways, I see no bright future for this country, for the experiment it represented for over 250 years, and for ourselves, who will have slit our own throats.

__Part I__ of this "poem," if indeed that is the correct term, raises the issue and the research approach adopted to study and then recommend possible solutions. __Part II__ is a critical look at the reasons – politically correct or otherwise – that have been suggested. And __Part III__ is something of an indictment of those who closed their minds and make their choices through an active and for many ongoing commitment to their new philosophy - ignorance. They deserve the blame for they have abandoned the basic principles on which this country was founded and put the rest of us – and some might say many across the world – at risk.   If indeed there was a myth of America, it has been seriously tarnished through their actions.

There is a disease, long known to mankind

Infectious, pernicious, its advanced stages affect the mind

Fostered since childhood, no vaccine is yet known

Its forms may vary though are most often home grown

Some survive, though how we can speculate

Even with intensive care, help often comes too late

It warps perceptions, turning the complex into the plain

Its symptoms appear early, but cause little pain

A mysterious ailment. Why is it so?

I could share our research, or would you rather not know?

Depending on location, it appears contagious

Some of the opinions that emerge are truly outrageous

There is some social stigma, so we speak only in general terms

A national epidemic, its presence is fet in places where no one learns

One side helped in a time of distress

The other sought only to make a mess

Memories are short or were some not paying attention

When the time came to be grateful, there was no mention

Instead they embraced the side that sought their demise

How is it that they voted against themselves, how is that wise?

Others focus on geographical location

Where historically to some causes there is a serious dedication

To some principals that should have been resolved long ago

But somehow they've held on and continued to grow

And then there is the issue of economic stagnation

Along with competition from abroad there has been and will be further automation

For too long we've ignored realities that were soon to arrive

And typically, we chose to just assume the present would continue to thrive

We've studied children to know how they learn

Each one is different, generalization are indeed a concern

We've concluded what everyone already knew

Studies are likely their results to skew

Wanting to find a simple single solution

We've once again called upon our friend devolution

We simplify and condense to make it easy to study

And exclude anything that might make the results muddy

And if the conclusions don't match our goals

We either don't publish or in the methodology poke holes

Or better yet, stick to the current standard line

Mention the study in passing and everything will be fine

But if you want to pursue a career in social research it's best to know

Be careful that your own bias - the equivalent of ignorance - will sooner or later show

I point this all out, for together it forms a whole

If we lose sight of this unity, we'll have fractured the goal

So many threats lie waiting for a chance

To insert their own objectives into the dance

But if the ones whose role it is to protect what's true

If they fail in their task, be they many or few

The essential pillar of this land of ours

Will forfeit all of its powers

Leaving us in a place we can't even conceive

For ignorance lives by its purpose - to deceive

PART II

Returning to the issue at hand

There is indeed a problem sweeping the land

We spend more money on education per child than any other nation

So what's going on with the educational degradation?

We can blame the teachers, they are on the front line

Their unions have been weakened so that should be fine

What reasons do they offer why they can't manage classes of fewer than 20

It will take some explanation to convince me of any

I fear it comes down to where the problem has always been

A culture that doesn't value education is headed for the bin

It is indeed values that matter

Setting aside all the peripheral patter

Look at those groups which have done well

I won't mention any names, but it's easy to tell

Of course other factors play a serious role

But life is a challenge and will take its toll

Perhaps the first lesson is to set aside

And from certain realities no longer hide

Here's another one sure to displease

This one is more a psychological disease

Parents matter, they prepare their children to lear

By teaching them to listen and focus, not to churn

Concentration is an acquired skill

Not a medical condition requiring a pill

We've thrown money at the problem, it looks good in the press

But rarely has it contributed to solving the mess?

Pointing out privilege indeed creates a political competition

It feeds the problem, and doesn't help its rendition

Linkage, enticements, punishment or exclusion

To focus on these things is to feed a delusion

Displacing the blame onto those over whom one has no control

Better to start with oneself, that's the quickest goal

Then there's a favorite, the matter of self esteem

How does one acquire such a thing and what does it mean?

No one should ever be always put down

Such treatment never produced a smiled, but many a frown

Distribution of empty awards fools no one at all

They rmay aise a child up for a moment, while simultaneously setting up the fall

What is given and not earned is flimsy at best

And telling them they are great when they fail a test

Is a crime against reality, for that's where we live

If the failure came from an illusion of a refusal to give

To put in the time and prepare for success

Now we're taking self-esteem, more solid, not less

Psychologists, doctors, specialists of all kinds

Pretend they can look deeply into children's minds

To do so requires a faculty are easy to find

Sadly to their own limitations that are blind

Does it happen often or more likely not]

Making believe only confuses the plot

Too much advised, if not truly inspired

Can provoke a result that would not be desired

Their advice can eat away at a parent's want to discern

And the child's true issues how can they learn?

Who spends more time with your child than you alone

Who knows them better if not you – they live in your home

A parent attentive, curious and committed to their task

If uncertain for some advice they may ask

But experts seduced by their own position and expertise

Should be careful to avoid an insidious disease

If an expert spreads confusion while imposing their views

Advice of this kind can only be bad news

In the face of these factors, though studied, what have we found?

I fear the most basic of causes suffer from having no political safe ground

So what do we do? What we have always done

Create a new program with funding and claim a home run?

If the trend we have seen over these many years

End up being the truth behind all of our fears

As other nations progress, we continue our decline

So perhaps, if not too late, I think it's time

Native intelligence can vary, we're all not the same

And not everyone can be the best in all things and expect to win every game

So let's back up a few steps and reset the clock

And place ourselves in the witness dock

Each child is different and will learn at their own pace

Each one will have strengths and weakness, life isn't a race

Pitting them against one another in an adversarial way

It may work for a few, but will also drive too many away

Like any good coach, it takes time to know

How to look at a child and learn as they grow

Standardization may help experts who speak

Though their contribution to me look disappointingly weak

To learn, a child needs the confidence to dare

Into the face of a mystery they need to stare

To believe they have the means to figure it out

And if they get stuck, explain, don't shout

Neither patronize, nor always seek the simplest way

Taking on what's difficult first, more will always pay

Watch the confidence grow, not the test results of one day

Acknowledge some of yourself in the child, don't just think it but say

It starts in the home, where love and security are to be found

A parent that's present is one that is emotionally around

If parents embrace failure, feeling they themselves have lost

What a tragic legacy they leave to their children, one that will exact a terrible cost

Or what if they cling to ambition, parsing the blame

Wanting their children to succeed at all costs and salvage the name

Better perhaps, but still not the best

Life for a child is not about aceing every test

Winning is part of life, but so it is to fail

To pick oneself up, to hoist again the sail

An essential lesson about life, what it says is spoken true

So when failure arrives, they will know what to do

Some children are born into families that know

Success is not wealth, and it will show

If a parent has learned in life what is real

The children will know why it's wrong to lie and steal

To earn is to possess what no other can take

It's how real men and women, parents can make

To know the value only the mind can bring

Nourished by example, success it will bring

But how can society teach this to those?

Who have weathered the travails of life and its many blows

No one wants to point a finger at those who vote

So money becomes the answer once again, learned by rote

We spend more and more and get less and less

We try different things and have created a mess

One nation requires one value system that ensures

That's broad enough so that it endures

Tolerance is good, indulgence is bad

To give too much without effort was a fad

Education is an opportunity, a chance to succeed

No guarantee can be based solely on need

Look on your children with eyes loving, ready for the long haul

The progress will be variable, moments of acceleration, others will stall

But faith in your child, constant and sure

Is the healthiest diet, organic and pure

Quick solutions, more money, another program that's new?

We've been there before and that's how we knew

Enough to say stop, let's talk about blame

Parenting is the key and must be the MVP in the game

Teach the parents and the children will grow

To be a parent on needs both to learn and to know

To learn how to watch and how to see

And how a good person oneself to be

To know is a matter of trusting oneself

It's not a quick fix or can be bought off the shelf

It involves taking a risk, and placing a bet

That you can provide and your child's needs will be met

Don't dwell onyour failures, you've entered a new place

Mistakes of the past, if you've learned from them, won't count
in this race

It's a new game for you hold a life in your hands

The life of your child, on you their future stands

An honor, a responsibility, a lifelong task

You say it just happened, that you did not ask

There are no easy passes or pardons to use

Like it or not, to have this child you did choose

If you fail in this most honorable task

The rest of your life, 'why" you will ask?

That's the wonder of reality, it forces us to see

What was, what is, and if we get it right, what will be

PART III

Now comes the part we'd all rather avoid

For it speaks to how a national consensus was destroyed

North versus south was one way we split in the past

We know how that ended, but its consequences still last

Then there was coastal, east and west

Seen to be privileged and arrogant by the rest

The effete had the money, the power and influence

But it was from the heartland that the spirit of America went
hence

We survived each episode at considerable cost

The edifice of state was chipped but not lost

The latest crack is not geographical

But has proven its value as a weapon tactical

Ignorance reveals many things

It relieves anger, but nothing of value it brings

It speaks only the language of "I don't want to know"

As it feeds off disaffection, watch it grow

A democracy has but a few basic needs

An educated population aware of its historical deeds

The real ones, not those we create and enshrine in myths

We need engaged citizens, not a few monoliths

Then there's the matter of what makes us who we are

It's carried us for a long time and taken us far

For America is based on an idea and not some family line

It's something to be proud of, worth preserving over time

Children need a parent or a king to decide in their place

To rule a people and define their race

Diversity, inclusion require thought

And sadly it's taken our kind centuries to be taught

So when some 60 million Americans made their choice

I wonder if contained in their collective voice

Was more a message of complaint, anger expressed

I understand that they find themselves now in circumstances distressed

In supporting a person who embodies no Americas ideals

Except perhaps our acquisitive nature which never heals

They closed their eyes to each man's reality

And embraced an ignorance too often encountered in our history

To choose to not know is to fail the nation

To support mean spirited policies is an offense to creation

To ignore the crimes show we continues to impose

And the graft and corruption like some weed that grows

If born blind, one deserves no blame

Every effort should be made to help them be in the game

But if, on the other hand, ignorance causes one to become intellectually blind

To continue to feed only junk food to a resentful mind

To ignore the forces that defines our reality

Makes for a selfish citizen who has abandoned his role in democracy

I find no satisfaction in being so abrupt

But what they have done managed to disrupt

Not just for now, but possibly for years to come

I hope when this President leaves those who support him will see what they've done

TAKING SIDES

September. 2018

I have a friend who I have known for awhile. Recently, he revealed much of his situation to me. At first, it seemed everything was clear, that he knew he was stuck, but wanted to find his way out of the compromise he had elaborated during his childhood, and which he had continued to employ into his forties. The past few years saw a rupture in the delicate balance he was living. He took a break from his profession, supporting himself in ways his conventional background it was much more than that.

To meet him socially, one would assume a relatively well adjusted man in his 40s who seemed to prefer living life as if he was in his 30s. His romantic attachments were superficially adequate, but the more I

came to know him, the more I realized what was wrong. He could trust no one.

The younger of two sons, an immigrant father and a religious mother, there was a fundamental imbalance in the family. Having grown up in less than ideal financial circumstances during the Depression, his mother was determined that men were supposed to not only work hard but succeed. Towards this goal, she bullied every male in the famiiy. Though small in stature, her mission gave her an overpowering presence, to the point where they all feared her wrath And it was not a simple correction There was such fire, such venom in her remonstrances that the father withdrew into his own world, the older son erected a thick high wall where he lived on the other side from his mother. But this man, being the youngest, found himself alone and terrified.

In her rage to succeed, the mother would identify any potential flaw, inflate it to the point when, as a child, he would be sent to be tested to see if everything was alright the point being was he capable of succeeding. Being of a milder, sweet nature, she implicitly decided that he would be her 'daughter,' and essentially let him know that he could not leave he. As in many marriages, fathers will develop a close relationship with his daughter, as the ideal woman, while the mothers, often feeling abandoned emotionally by their husbands, will see solace with a son. In both instances, the damage to the child can be severe.

Within this context, an interesting phenomenon emerged, one I had observed elsewhere. Whereas my friend wore something of a mask which contained many of the qualities he felt lacking in himself, the real he was well concealed, and let out on only the rarest occasions. The former could be selfish, a bit nasty, and inconsiderate. Qualities you might ask? When it came to dealing with his mother, these were indeed the qualities which allowed him to assert his independence to some degree. But the latter, the real he, lived in a world of fear, always looking over his shoulder, anxious and incapable of trusting another person enough to actually commit to them.

As they grew up, these two allies who had worked together towards compatible goals began to diverge. Each one took on a mission, and would alternate whenever the over overstepped their role. This was not a case of multiple personality disorder. In fact, they were each aware of the other.

The more assertive one totally identified with the mask. He was a ladies man, said to be wild, a big partier. Always ready to go out and have a good time, he led the life of a student . His prime directive was to "be happy," and prevent the original one from straying from his protection. But this became too confining, too contrary to his desire to escape the prison his protector had built for him. And so he would go back and forth between the two, each one intervening when the other went too far.

I would point out to him the inevitability of one winning out over the other, and that the loser might, in fact, be himself. He needed to choose a side and commit to it, acting exclusively in accordance with his inner needs and desires. He was the real person. The other was a mask but a mask that was gaining strength and control every day.

He had a few choice phrases, banal perhaps in appearance, but painfully lucid and prophetic. Whenever he would open up and begin to trust, he would say "…I just can't get out of my own way." No sooner than *the very next day, the assertive one would show up. As I pressed him, he would chastise his alter ego saying "I'm so weak."*

This is a poem about this constellation and how it worked. I had seen it in another friend and knew, if this growing gap between them continued to develop, who would lose.

We had one friend in common, and I shared with him and his wife my concerns. They dismissed the gravity of the situation, no seeing – I believe not wanting to see – behind the mask. He made them laugh, h was fun and enterprising, and always good company. Without realizing it, they contributed to making him a prison of his own creation, the man, who was in fact a boy, living behind the mask.

Sadly, several months later, and though he gave no warning, he took his own life. At the funeral, there were four eulogies. In spite of all his "friends," no one knew who he really was. And our mutual friend, in informing me of where the funeral was to be held, indirectly and inappropriately told me that if I was going to say "I told you so," that I should not come. Clearly, none of his wanted to see his pain because they were all hiding from their own. The only thing I said to this person was that none of his friend cared enough to see what he revealed to me.

To have the courage to see and feel

To know what's true and makes things real

Though painful at first, it alone can heal

Therein lies the essential deal

Lives are built on messages sent, stone by stone

Creating an image that is rarely one's very own

A servitude begun from the time one is born

Others will choose the clothing that's worn

Man or woman, who holds the key?

Parents early on decide how yourself you will see

The dragon breathes her deadly fire

I've come now to see which of your parts would expire

No knight, nor father nor even older brother

No one came to your aide, nor protected you from the devouring mother

Claimed you, she did, as her own

Such was the cloud beneath which you have grown

Saddled with disabilities that were never true

From the world of men, she separated you

Though on the outside, allowed to grow

That part that makes of you a man no one let you know

You tried to rebel in so many ways

Early on, you found a compromise to get through the days

Like most compromises, it came at a cost

From one you became two, though in the end more would be
lost

Split in two now, life lived as a contradiction

The years went by in dereliction

The pillars on which every man relies

Have been nibbled away by so many illusions and lies

Each one a tumor, out of control, unchecked

Might there come a day when It's too late to correct ?

I've met so many wanting to believe

One part says yes, the other says leave

But out from the shadows another arrives

You ignored its strength and on what it thrives

Feeding off the truer core

Into your heart it continues to bore

The pretext, only a losing compromise

No one suspected its strength or its size

Stealthy it waits for every inevitable opening

Only new complications would it bring

Longing to trust, but fearing the same

This is how it became a unwinnable game

Vulnerable yet guarded every hour of the day

Fearing those harsh words you knew she would say

Each one chipping away at your soul

Love can take many forms, yet hers had but one goal

Complicit you are, I think you know

When we settle for so little, how can we grow?

For reasons no one can ever explain

On your side Life faithful for a time still will remain

Watching over them, sending opportunity their way

When She asks what will you say?

Will you repeat the same answers asking nothing new?

There are always new questions waiting for you

To find an ally, a friend for support

To put an end to this battle, and the struggle abort

To give you the means to believe again, to hope

And find more than just another way to cope

If you open your eyes and see that luck exists

If you find it in you to step up and your life not to miss

This time the choice has a voice

Do you still know how to rejoice?

This voice comes from the outside

Until now you do both – come and hide

The truer self has moments sincere

When it can set aside your too familiar fear

Yet the warrior, the servant whose task requires

To hold on fast, hunker down and stoke the fires

It tells you as always a better place cannot be true

There is no one to trust in this world waiting for you

With each breath you take of the fresh air

There appears a hint that you might start to care

No sooner it appears, that's how soon it is gone

The battle for your soul rages on

There are times when potential gives way to what's real

How long does it take for someone to learn how to feel?

For each time it seems, the past does prevail

And when it does, all is forgotten, and it's all been to no avail

That friend who fights by your side

He will do what you'll let him so you won't be carried off by the tide

He knows what it's like, his own battle he won

There is purpose to friendship, not just fun

This constant back and forth must cost you dear

And not just you, this too must be clear

The trust you desire yet fear each day

Must also be received for it to stay

Instead of a skirmish followed by a truce

It's time to set the wild horses loose

To discover what to others is so very clear

And to actually let someone in, to let them be near

There are not many whose trust can be found

Everyone is looking to take, with too few givers around

So see what you have, get out of your own way

I know there exists a chance for you to finally say

"I belong to me and no other can claim

I am here and though you gave me my name

You've taken too much, now it's my time

I have but one life and I finally want to make it mine."

THE OTHER

This is one of my hybrid situations where I had a good friend who lived in the neighborhood. He was a casual acquaintance with whom, over time, we had become friends. As often happens, for I am truly interested, he started opening up to me about himself. Though he appeared to be a somewhat overage twenty something who was actually closer to 50 than 30, his life had begun to seriously come apart.

On a break from his profession for going on 3 years with no apparent intention of resuming a conventional professional life in view, he filled his days with diverse distractions. His stated goal was to be happy.

Not long after I met him, a three year relationship with his girlfriend ended, much to his surprise. The reasons were not specific, though they were clear. She was a troubled individual from a very neurotic family, and he was your classic case of Peter Pan. He portrayed the rupture as being deeply troubling, but it didn't take him long before he found another inaccessible, inappropriate woman for casual sex which, after a brief period, ended. He had less conventional relationships before, during and after, but he would always feel obligated to return to a situation more in line with what his parents might approve of. Interestingly, he would go back and forth between a rebellious attitude, only to revert back to a more conventional one, before going too far. In any case, there would be no "too far" for him, because his personal issues would not allow him to ever trust someone enough to actually let them in.

Though younger than the friend, there were certain cultural similarities which created a certain sympathy between the two, which played a role in the friend's perseverance. But before long, the friend found himself implicated in a drama far more complex that one might have suspected initially.

I have revealed certain aspects of this story, but have been very careful to render it impossible for anyone to identify the players. That being said, my version of this experience is subjective, however convinced I may be of its accuracy in fact and motivation.

Why share this? Because it is the second example – the first being related in The Leftovers of God's Anger – The Chris Chronicles – of the appearance of a sort of alter ego, emerging spontaneously from the unconscious to come to the aid of the individual. And unfortunately, the outcome of the interaction required in the first instance, the victory of this alter ego over the original individual. Though not identical by any means, the phenomenon is real, little explored, but certainly worthy of consideration.

A child that grows up in a world unsuited

Something profound occurs; its sense of self is diluted

Shifted by force from its rightful place

Incomplete yet told they are ready, for life is a race

They hear voices citing their every flaw

Can confidence ever be found when living under such a maw

Of some mother bear or father cruel

A child needs protection, not another troubled tool

But nature foresaw situations like this

To find a way to survive when things go amiss

A mask is one answer, to assume the part

And try at first, not to take it to heart

The words of disapproval whose purpose contains

Perhaps some caring, but carries far more stains

Those of the indelible kind

That will mark forever a child's mind

For a parent who hates themselves for failures they see

A child and their future represents an opportunity

To rewrite indirectly their own history

Can this be true when the life unintended is imposed on someone not free?

An innocent brought into this world, unformed and wild

Is this not the best way to consider a child?

In need of a loving hand, and a vision that's clear

To point the best way forward and banish the fear

But instead of a road to a life of their own

Another mission was selected for them, as yet unknown

One message they hear for which there is no defense

"You're wrong, I'm right" - of this position can a child make any sense?

This declaration, on what is it built

But a threat unimagined, bundled in guilt

Under such coercion what child would not wilt?

They stand there pretending to acquiesce, but after hide under their quilt

At night, alone, when no one can see

To dream how life otherwise might be

And so begins a journey few speak of

Of an unsuspected ally to pick up the glove

To create another, one brave and strong

In the place of the weak who fear to never belong

Born of necessity, a fantasy takes shape

Instead of a child, appears a man with a cape

Why not? Fantasies begin in the land of dreams

A place where there are no fears or nocturnal screams

Nurtured each day to make them grow

A secret 'other" that no one else will know

He looks like me, it's close enough

But with different expressions and an attitude that's tough

Some might say I've grown moody, others something is wrong

They know me as weak, but he is strong

A split begins to form, of one becoming two

In tandem over time, together they grew

But strength was not all that separated these boys

One gave in, the other owned his toys

When old enough, with the mask firmly in place

In secret the Other would venture forth, but left no trace

With stealth their places did they exchange

The point being not to derange

But rather to step in to defend his original half

The change in his manner made no one laugh

For he would let no one claim control

Nor would he allow trust to be the goal

For it was a pact not to be shared

Otherwise, he would never have dared

Living two lives, different in every way

At first it worked, or so I heard him say

Slowly his role began to shift

From purely defensive, to a more assertive fit

And as the Other seemed to each time claim more room

He wanted a life of his own, a different cloth made necessary a
different loom

It took quite some time before things fell apart

Relationships came and went, but were based on a false start

They might last awhile, but his choices concealed one fact

Both knew it would end through a coincidental act

Or when one realized they were wasting their time

If they took too long, he would give them a sign

A reason to say it was over, things had gone too far

Back to where he started, no motor ever came with his car

He found a friend who tried to reveal

What was going on in the hope he could heal

The first would listen and bemoan his fate

But a short time after, the Other would have him clear his plate

For more than a year he managed to pursue

The friendship, for it was something new

It didn't take long before the Other joined the mix

And began the back and forth common to his usual tricks

Dealing with one person at a time

Can be trying and can work out fine

But when one become two, both living in the same head

The chance for someone authentic to emerge is close to dead

Stubborn he was, this friend incisive

But the more he insisted, the more the Other grew decisive

Until it reached a point where harm entered the scene

No one suspected how far the Other would go, and just how mean

He fell down drunk in his shower one night

Blood everywhere, it was quite a site

He managed to call 911, quickly they came

Before losing consciousness, he could give them his name

It took more than 2 months for him to feel

The Other was proud of his coup, for him a good deal

But the injured party continued to try

As the friend pressed onward to show him why

Why a freak accident when he'd entered a thousand times

One could almost hear the Other preparing other land mines

And sure enough, once he was healed

He fell once again, once more the truth revealed

He claimed he had friends, with a life that was busy

Though he said he took care of himself, he was too often dizzy

As the Other upped the ante, so did the friend

Seeing through the lies and the games, he fear how it would end

One more time, he suffered an injury important enough

That he would have to move in with parents with some of his stuff

The friend warned him of what might come of this

To remain with his parents for too long, and if his freedom he did not miss

Would mean but one thing and that things is not good

The other had gained the upper hand living in the parent's
neighborhood

So began for the friend a reflection on his case

Refusing to abandon what was becoming a race

Was a flaw of his own that he saw revealed

In his friend whose fate was looking more and more sealed

There's no telling at this point what the outcome will be

But one thing I for sure, this man will never be free

The friend also learned why it was so hard

To say goodbye to someone who would never leave his
backyard

Another example of how we manage to make ourselves blind

To the things that go counter to a state of mind

For he had known a version of this friend's difficult task

But he had managed it well, so when he felt this man did ask

For help, implicitly, for to be open and clear

Would require of him courage to get past his fear

Stay tuned if you want to, I'll provide an update

But I fear for my friend, it may well be too late

WHEN ONE BECOMES TWO BECOMES ONE

November 2018

I wrote this poem as I watched a friend of mine, during the course of almost two years, first split himself into two entities, and then progressively drown himself (figuratively) in a sea of lies. I had seen this phenomenon, this creation of an alter ego, in another person that I wrote another book about – The Leftovers of God's Anger. Though different in the manner in which the conflict between the two sides engaged, as was the outcome, the similarities were too striking to ignore

Both were victims of abusive parents. In the first instance, this abuse manifested itself by a complete and total emotional abandonment. This time, the parents, the mother in particular, was convinced she was doing everything she could to ensure her son's success. Unfortunately, the method she used was a mix of a constant flow of "constructive" criticism, a message that he was somehow inadequate, and a vituperative tongue which transformed her words into razor blades - a terrifying figure. She was very present in his life, in the manner of the Mother Who Devours Her Own Children, for this is exactly what she did.. Her wrath was inescapable, to the point that I often observed him anxious, though for no obvious reason. Nothing he did could ever be good enough. She had done this to his father, who gave up when my friend was still quite young. And the older brother – he left for the West Coast, and made sure not to come back too often. My friend was to be the sacrificial son, given over to the mother, who preferred to see him die than to let him go. A cruel observation indeed. Yet a conclusion so obvious, so clear, should pity for a grieving mother dismiss her role? Feel sorry for her if she felt remorse. And from what I could see, there wasn't much at all. It was his fault – not hers.

He found no support in his father, who had become himself an object of the mother's constant litany of his inadequacies. I hesitate to use the classical term of castration, though that could apply. Rather, she was not evil, and provided more validation – not often of the appropriate kind – than the father. As a child, this man came to hate his father for failing to protect him from the dragons fire.

Lacking the means to defend himself, there was but one possible response – rebellion. But with a terrifying mother, it had to be of an indirect, more passive nature. He was not a masochist in the sense that he never relished her reprimands. But he would always deny her the complete satisfaction she demanded. His academic and professional choices were honorable, but in his mother's eyes, below what she wanted. And there was the matter of trust, for he could trust neither parent, since one abused him (however well intentioned) and the other failed to protect him.

His relationships reflected a profound ambivalence which found its true expression in this rebellious alter-ego. His original self was someone who, had he been able to" get out of his own way" – his words – would have lived a very different, more stable life. Plagued by this constant fear that nothing he could do would ever be good enough, he was dogged by anxiety. Though not to the point of being incapacitated, for seen from the outside, he appeared quite normal. Yet he could never let his guard down, never truly let go. He was lucid, and tried In his own way to find some solution. As often happens, frustration can redirect a good intention down a more primal path. It takes an unusually thoughtful person to see this, and allow it to recover a more positive expression. Unfortunately, his alter ego saw things quite differently.

A child of a child who saw themselves as weak and in need of defending, emerged from his unconscious someone who was quite the opposite of his host. Selfish, self-serving, rather unfeeling, even cruel at times, he had one mission. To be strong enough to prevent any enduring trust to develop between his weaker side and anyone else. In fact, his approach was to always find a way to disqualify whatever positive initiative might be taken. And he was good at what he did.

There was a constant battle between the two sides: one wanted to break free and claim his life for himself; the other thought only to preserve him at all costs. Being friends with him was a challenge until I realized what was going on. Though fully aware of the two sides, he could never gain control over his defender. The constant back and forth between openness, followed by a refusal to see anything in a positive light inexorably evolved towards the end of the friendship. Once the alter ego won, the outcome had become inevitable.

As I often told my friend, there is always a choice, though sometimes beyond the reach of the individual. Here, I believe he had no faith in his own strength, his own ability to simply say 'no more.' And the appeal of the security he found hiding behind his alter ego, the weakness he came to embrace in all its manifestations were too tempting. The alter-ego was a master liar, capable of turning any truth that got close to the truth on its head. Though I would call him out on it once I realized this was his way, he would drop one lie and create another.

It was the lies he came to tell himself that finally will have won the day. I had hoped someday there would be another rebellion, a real one, for as I told him when he would talk about his self-esteem issues in an attempt to convince me that he was weak and helpless, that I saw more potential in him than he saw in himself. When that is the problem, the problem is not the problem, but the problem with the problem.

Too many words are spoken

To hide what has been broken

Indulge it for too long

And what should be right will go wrong

Discretion indeed can provide

An unhealthy reason to hide

We fear to rock the boat

When only truth can keep it afloat

So fragile have we all grown?

That we forget what should be known

And what is known should be shared

Why then are we so scared?

Of ourselves? Are we now but a mask?

The partial answer must be yes, since I ask

We may claim the reason is others to please

Or is there an epidemic of some other, insidious disease?

When we can no longer know for sure

When we've told so many lies impure

The one we seek to appease

Is the carrier of the disease

The one who lives emprisoned deep inside

How much of ourselves we seek to hide

Ashamed, afraid and insecure

If too long left untreated can there still be found a cure?

How did this happen, we can't bear to see?

The full and honest truth – our own reality

So full of secrets dark and truths unspoken

Could we be anything else but afraid and broken?

A subtle illusion. More distance each one creates

The greater the distance, the more one hates

So that over time one becomes two

The original one and the one new

Improved, molded to resemble whom we think we should be

In so doing we take another step away from our own reality

If the new and improved grows too strong

To whom will this first person really belong?

In the end, one must ultimately prevail

And if it's the mask, then ourselves we fail

Abandoned the fight, delegated it all

Leaving us of little consequence and small

No soul, no spirit, no courage to defend

What will we say to our children by this message we send?

Believing we teach them to themselves be true

How can we make believe they never knew?

But what is done unknowingly, is done none t he same

Does it not change the nature of the game?

How much time before no one knows where to find?

The way back home to some state of a natural mind

If all that remains is to disparage and cast doubt

Will anyone in the future understand what Life is about?

We may be alive, but how will it be?

If what is lost will define our new reality?

Disputatious, resentful, lost and afraid

Is this to be the result of those great plans long ago laid?

Was there ever a chance the dream might come to be?

Or were they too blind a future they could not see

To inspire is a chance, not a promise kept

Into the unkown many have lept

We can keep the promise, and stay the course

Or get lazy and lost and unaware, from ourselves divorce

Simple, as always, some truths are to see

If we look with our hearts and our eyes, clarity can be

But embrace blindness, turn your eyes away

And there will come to be a very different day

There is light, there is darkness, a void in between

Darkness lies beneath our feet, damp, wet and mean

Above us shines a light, lies revealed through with clarity

A way to live better requires a good dose of honesty

Those demons that plague every day and night

That show discord and distract from that which is right

Strong they become if we let them remain

Only the light can remove their persistent stain

Which will it be then, which will we choose?

Will fear win out and what will we lose?

Or from within the darkness will something emerge?

And save us from ourselves and this primal urge?

To cling to the past, afraid to face it down

To let in invade every home, every town

Though a haven it was so long ago

Now a prison it's become, this you need know

At the time, perhaps it was the best you could do

A child lacks strength, and its allies are few

The solution of erecting high walls to hide behind

Can have a long lasting effect on the mind

But the years have past, the price has been high

It's time to rise up and look to the sky

To imagine the future, let it be like a screen

And there catch a glimpse of what can still be your dream

This vision is the road we follow, though not written in stone

Where this leads is a place where our souls we disown

It's waiting somewhere around the bend

But there is still time for us to mend

But with each day we let the lies live

It's never too late to learn to give

Like stones placed one at a time

Telling ourselves and each other everything is fine

Continue as before, though problems arise

There will always be another to blame and despise

Denial, that old friend, he who can make us all blind

Who can confuse every issue and change our mind

Well practiced are his tricks, invoked every day

But I see the cost of what he takes away.

So there it is, I'm done for now

I'd rather speak of other things if only the world would allow

I wish there was comfort in leaving it in your hands

But there isn't, and that's where today it all stands

Another dark warning? I grow tired them too

I wish I could offer a vision fresh and new

But then I would be guilty of that which I warn

From the grasp of this prison of our own creation we can still be reborn

THE DAMAGE

November 2018

Little did I realize how premonitory this, and some of the other poems, were to prove. It also shows how perceptive we can be – and still not grasp the full extent of what our unconscious selves reveal. My friend took his own life little more than one month after I wrote this poem. I feared a progressive deterioration, but never did I imagine he would choose to leave so soon. I doubt he knew himself until the very evening when, as can happen, an epiphany arrives. Did he catch a glimpse of a better place, that happy place he longed to find? He said he didn't want material things or any other conventional sign of success.   I felt that route had been taken from him early on.

And so he wore a mask of a happy go lucky, fun, party type, wild in his search for enjoyment, yet oddly unsuccessful here. Others didn't notice, and he had only begun since we met to realize the extent of the war for his soul that was raging inside. He wore a mask to mollify his mother and her ambitions for so long he thought it was he. And then it hit him. That thing that had been pushing him to have a secret life, was actually himself, the real one, desperately trying to survive.

He had lots of friends, he had parents involved in his life, and a brother with whom he claimed to be close. So how is it that no one say this coming? I did. And it was obvious. Were these people who supposedly love him, who had known his for many years, so wrapped up in their own lives that as long as he didn't say anything, they had full licence not to see.

In the six months prior to his demise, he had three serious accidents, all the result of slipping in the shower, tripping on the steps to his building, or twisting his ankle playing football. The first two were quite serious, requiring hospitalization and a lengthy recovery. Was this not a sign of some message trying to get through? I thought so. But the obvious, the superficial can often provide a useful cover for what we'd rather not see.

And that was my impression of this collective lie they were all supporting – not just about my friend. The lie was the collective image, the myth they created about themselves as members of a tribe. As long as everyone towed the line, kept the lie going, solidarity would prevail. But to deviate from the core image, to distinguish oneself in any way, would constitute a serious challenge to the group.

And so they buried my friend celebrating a life he didn't really have, recounting the good times he never enjoyed, and sending him off without much sense of the tragedy that had just occurred. He didn't really count for them as the man he was. He counted only insofar as he could contribute to supporting everyone's reassuring message that we're all fine – just fine.

Early on I sensed there was more to this person than just a good time. Part of him tried at first to divert my attention to other things, events in his life, his business, his friends. But the scent was fresh and easy to follow if one actually cared.

Though at times difficult to see oneself through the eyes of another, but for real. I saw more than the pain and loneliness. I also saw someone who could have been, should have been given more of a chance than he was. The youngest of two sons, his mother chose him to keep for her own. All of this was not hard to expose. And I also saw someone truly worthwhile.

As in fairy tales which convey so much truth about life's journey, there is a hero, a challenge, a quest for some great prize. Often, when at its most perilous, when it seems the hero is lost, there arrives a friend, an ally, often even a helpful, magical animal. And with their assistance, the hero overcomes the obstacle and continues his journey.

At the moment when this aide arrives, the hero is often despondent, having seen more the difficulty and less his ability to meet it. He has a choice: accept the aide and risk losing or winning, or reject the help and embrace defeat. This is the critical moment which determines the outcome.   More than the source of the problem, more than its difficulty. It is at this moment that the hero must realize that this help comes not from the outside, but from his own unrecognized inner resources. To face the challenge without them is to lose for sure. But to embrace the unsuspected potential lying within, to forget about what's happening outside and focus on what's coming from inside, offers the best, if not the only, chance for success.

That's the problem with problems. I have played that role in the lives of several people – the friend, helper, ally, even magical animal. I believe in them because it is what anyone who cares must do. Their potential was not some fantasy. It was real though I often seemed to be the only one willing to point it out. But life offers no guarantees, which explains why too many give up, preferring the certainty of defeat over the risk of not succeeding.

Help we can provide. But the choice remains always with the hero. And that choice is the first and most important obstacle to overcome. Sadly, it is not given to everyone to see that hope comes from courage, and courage from strength. And strength? Strength can be seeded – indeed should be seeded – by one's family. But most of all, strength comes from being tested, of seeking the Golden Fleece, of discovering through the challenge, who one really is. Spared this definitive experience – often by choice – one can only fall back onto arrogance, hubris, and deceitful fantasy. It's that fateful mirror, perhaps the Gorgon's meaning – to look into the eyes of truth one can eitherfind oneself, or be frozen in stone, for though the appearance may seem real, the substance is a facsimile..

How is it some learn how to care?

Willing they are to seek out and dare

When others flee their feelings in fright

Is there one explanation for this blight?

Replaced are the values of the heart

Though so many seem to feel apart

They may know why they recoil

They may even know how this will spoil

It's not the fear of being hurt

Nor Is it having been treated like dirt

Vulnerability? That may be true

A fear of intimacy, now there's a clue

Is it trust, or having been betrayed?

That's made their hearts cold and staid

They've learned how to take, but not to give

They speak of happiness, but are afraid to live

Commitment means a loss of control

Without another can one ever be whole?

Not a goal in a game that one can win

Is this perhaps not the original sin?

Those who strive to be self-aware

Know that life was not meant to be fair

For behind what may look like love

Resides an agenda hidden inside the glove

This word with which we season our lives

Can contain something else, something dark exists and thrives

Never mentioned for we fear its name

Yet clearly it is part of the game

Can it ever be revealed in broad daylight?

Would it lose its hold if it lived in plain sight?

Is that the true mystery when talk turns to love?

Will we ever see its face, know it purpose, this nameless thing never spoken of?

We all have secrets, legacies of the past

We can run from them as far and as fast

Until faced, they will outlast

A shadow over our lives they will cast

Hiding them only serves one end

A toxic message does it send

Fear who you really are

Become a what and you will go far

Splitting oneself in two might work for a time

Convincing others that everything is fine

As the gap continues to grow

Cracks in the façade will start to show

More energy required to keep the mask

Why it gets harder you begin to ask

The something will happen, a sign but from where

An eruption occurs and you start to care

Control is weaker, you wonder why

Tighten the screw, at the very least try

But it won't work, things look different now

What is going on, why and how?

These urges coming from who knows where

Suddenly tempted to actually dare

Inconsistent with what the mask requires

A conflict develops but no one retires

Finally this other piece has a name

His purpose singular, he's changed the game

The mask if fearful, can this other be tamed

Adversaries now, the mask is ashamed

Realizing what he has done

Before he just wanted a life made of fun

But not a war he truly begun

He wonders if it's too late, has he lost or won

Tired he grows of this struggle with no escape

He looks back in time, reviewing the tape

An abyss stares back at him, its mouth agape

And at the bottom lies a coffin covered in black crepe

It's empty for now, does that mean there is hope

What must he do if only for the moment to cope?

Panic sets in, double down on what worked before

Maybe he can make it to the exit door

He didn't know it was to be the last time

He would make the wrong choice, a sign

There was a chance, had he only thought of himself as a whole

From the jaws of defeat, a victory, a goal

And so he chose to leave the field

The weakness of masks will always yield

For they are meant to be more than an interface

Built, they were not, to run the full race

Masks are superficial things, they have no depth

Having only length and breadth

No substance, no real reason to endure

Neither values nor hopes of which they are sure

Lost is another soul, sacrificed to an empty God

They left half their lives to rot in the sod

Though choices exist, how many cannot believe

That no matter how tough, the right choice will relieve

Others can help, they can care

But this can work only if they dare

For this friend, this brother, this son

I wanted somehow to save this one

He tried as hard as he thought he could do

And though all the pieces were there to see in plain view

Weakness, once embraced offers no release

Leaving but one solution to find a too final peace

WORTHWHILE

January 2019

It was the evening of the day before New Years. I hadn't seen him for awhile and was surprised to receive his text message. There was nothing unusual about it. In fact it seemed to be lacking the usual ambivalence which haunted him. Most people took him to be wild, a little crazy in a good way, but anxious at times, and often controlling. very controlling. He had the ability to go in two opposite directions in close proximity, suggesting indecision or even chronic confusion. His friends used to attribute it to his frequent partying. How convenient for them.

The first two messages were friendly. But the third contained that easily recognizable edge that would characterize his alter ego. I called him out on it, as I always did. Mostly, it was to draw his attention to it for himself, as I had been doing for awhile. Being his friend was not always easy as how would bounce back and forth in the most predictable manner. Yet it was easy to rein him in – by teling the other one I wasn't interested in playing his games. I didn't hear back which was also not unusual.

Two days later, a mutual friend sent me a text with a link to a funeral home in Queens, but forgot to include the name of the deceased. As my friend had elderly parents, I first thought of them. But then I went cold inside. Could it be? I responded, and those fears I had been warning him about suddenly materialized. He had put an end to his life.

His mother found the body, so no one knows, nor will ever know, if he left a note. The first accounting was that he had taken too many Ambien 'by mistake." As he had been taking Ambien for awhile, the plausibility of that explanation was weak.

I had shared my concerns with this mutual friend in the past, encouraging him to help getting our friend sorted out for real. Superficially, he had his own thoughts, suggesting that our friend needed only to move to a larger apartment. Living in such a small space wasn't healthy – according to him. I wasn't able to get him to envision the nature and source of the problem.   To believe that his friend could be so sad, so unhappy in his life and so unable to break free from his family would have required that he take a similar look into his own heart. Groups of friends often share, even support, a common myth about the group and the individual who compose it.

To break ranks for the benefit of one member was not something the group would tolerate.

My friend was being held hostage not only by his family, but also by his group of friends, none of whom saw who he really was, nor cared to even look.

I went to the funeral and was shocked. Though there were some who expressed sadness, claimed they were devastated, by some means they had decided that they would celebrate his life rather than mourn it. "That's how he would have liked it." Really? I sat there watching, listening to the eulogies, with the saddest of feelings. In death as in life, it seemed I alone knew who he was, and was not. I felt honored that he, who trusted no one, came to trust me. I knew someone else who experienced something similar under very different circumstances, and wrote about it in another book –" The *Leftovers of God's Anger.*" It too was a tragic tale. I had tried there as well to help, to give this young man who had always been pusned away, unwanted, a sense of his own value – independent of what others thought. The last time I saw him, he said to me "I am soafraid of dying alone." And he walked off alone, with hardly anything to his name, into the dark night. That was over 2 years ago. I don't know for certain, but I think he too had decided to say goodbye – for good.

Both these people, fundamentally among the best people I have known, brought me to this book. I needed to try and make sense of why, when you offer someone the help they desperately need and want, they cannot take use it to take that final step to the other side. Their conviction, acquired throughout their childhood and beyond, went so deep, became so much a part of their identity, as to be impossible to alter it.

Problems are practical things, and always have solutions. They may not be ideal, nor resemble anything one might have desired. But there are always options. So why do most people categorically refuse them? What is the problem with problems? It's not the "what." It never is. It's always the "who." It's whether or not we can see ourselves through our own eyes rather than those of others that will determine whether or not we can ever reclaim ourselves, remove ourselves from the paths others have chosen for us, and enter the realm of risk that is life. The past is always certain and immovable. The future, by it's very nature, is unknown. We see it as rich with potential or fraught with insurmountable risk and danger. Therein lies the choice, the determining factor. That is the problem with problems.

Over the years I constituted a certain file

Composed of those who have come and gone into a pile

As I watched it grow bigger, wearing a world weary smile

Something was missing fundamentally leaving no place for denial

It became so obvious too rapidly

How all conversation had turned vapidly

Not in a way I thought I was superior

But because they were empty on the interior

Living a life where it is what we have that decides

Is that truly where the value we represent resides?

Was there ever a time when other things were known?

To be of importance, they must be shown

Whatever became of the "who" that we are?

Or is it just easier to lower the bar?

When things such as personal values, those handed down

When embraced, our own search is left to drown

No need to think any longer, to strive and to hope

With the future gone, it's the immediate satisfaction for which
we grope

In the dark, with eyes that never yearned to see

And to know it's what's inside that is truly me

I lost someone I cared for a few days ago

He took his own life for he feared to know

That he had a future, though hidden deep

Decisions made by a mother determined her son to keep

This one was to be for her alone, never set free

She took away any faith he had that he might one day be

Beaten down each and every day

Rather see him gone than let him walk away

So a mask he wore, his best means of defense

When caught in a circle that to him made no sense

The best he could do was resist passively

While giving her part of what she wanted, obsessively

For it was she who taught him money was all

While his nature was to be sweet and heed its call

Of others in need, to do good in that way

While he bore her assaults every day

A compromise is solution where no one can win

Sometimes it works, sometimes it's a sin

One can give up some things, though there is one rule to abide

Never abandon the field, and from your true self hide

To enter the cell, head down and defeated

With only a sentence so unfairly meted

There to languish, while trying to please

The world which cares little as forms a cancerous disease

One that eats away at organs vital

As progressively we sign away to ourselves the title

For him, a split had taken place

There emerged a different, yet familiar, face

One that was his, different, rich in the qualities he did lack

Through this other alone was he able to fight back

Of the two, the first was a prisoner for life

The other version feared nothing and carried a knife

Who learned to say no, never how to say yes

Armed with a resolve, he never had to guess

His mission was clear, trust no one, by this defined

This was a contract that would torment his mind

Having no power of his own to nourish any hope

His life became a juggling act of how to cope

As mother's assaults continued apace

There was father, though he'd taken himself out of the race

He too feared the dragon, worn down over time

No protector was he when she crossed the line

And a brother older, he ran away

Never a thought to help little brother, selfish that way

He who became the slave of Mother Dear

Who ruled like some immovable rock, spewingr flames of fear

The gap between his two sides grew wider over the years

While smiling outside, the inside never stopped shedding tears

For himself, unable to walk through an open door

Such was his fear, a hole in his courage it bore

A hole so deep, so wide, so impossible to cross

The sense of hopelessness grew apace, as well as the loss

Of hope, of desire, of having a chance

This was now a man with no partner to dance

For he was unable trust no one intimately

For that, one need trust oneself to survive vulnerability

In the last years of his life, a chance encounter arrived

Thankfully, a few embers had survived

The final battle began as the troops came to assemble

The formations on the field gave him cause to tremble

Two years ensued as the battle did rage

At times he was even dared to step out of his cage

His fear of trusting, while suspended, he realized

Had grown to proportions completely outsized

The mission impossible, the one from the past

The one he carried his whole life he saw at last

The line was there, he need only advance

But the other had allies, and left him no chance

That fatal night, though never made his intention known

A clear choice appeared, a subjective truth shown

Continue to struggle with no belief he could win

Or seize victory from defeat, and just give in

And that's what he did. He walked through his cell's door

For him life had become a hopeless chore

An affirmative act, in his eyes, he didn't lose

No more living a life, singing alone the blues

Making believe he was someone else, though offering rare clues

He noticed his friends didn't care enough. To them his pain would be news

He thought not of others, those few who cared

Funny how in this moment he finally dared

To think only of himself, he had a selfish side

In the end he'd always been alone, for others he never cried

If no one cared enough to see his pain

Why should he feed the lie, and here remain?

Though he knew someone did care

In the end he thought only to himself to be fair

What of this one person who he'd trusted the most?

That too he kept secret when safely he could finally coast

In a way, he tried to say goodbye

But it went unrecognized, he didn't really try

Thinking back it's as if part of him had already left

Almost invisibly did he walk away with not thought for the bereft

An exchange of text messages was had between the two

Of his intentions, only one of them knew

I've asked myself over and over again

I guess it's quite natural to revisit what had happened then

Who knows what it means to truly care?

When so much of another's life one had come to share

A bond forms that cannot be shaken

Only when the other is taken

Looking back, I realize it now

He just couldn't choose a side, he didn't know how

Reach out with one hand, take back with the other

Until the mask managed those few embers to smother

Those many years of solitude, of making believe

In his death he found peace, and the pain to relieve

How those who claimed to be his friends

Cared not enough to have seen his truth – and this is how it ends

The light went out, freed after too many tries

Too many moments of fear that did terrorize

I look at those many faces lying on the rejected pile

I say it out loud as I said it to him: here was someone worthwhile

Sad I am for his having given in

When I was still there and he could still win

Blame him I can't, though to me it was a sin

Though I know one can never know it all on the outside looking
in

Leave, I told him, and go to a place

Where he could throw off this cursed face

A place where he wasn't known

Where the one inside could have grown

Into the man he longed to be

But he had decided he would head for the sea

Too much to ask, too hard the task?

For one who only longed to but in the sun to bask

Of the misguided waste, the unholy compromise

The sum of too many hopeless tries

For he was someone who was fundamentally worthwhile

Never destined to be lost to the rejection pile

I will miss him for the trust he gave

There were moments when I felt I could save

This frightened boy in the body of a man

But in his heart of hearts, he had another plan

I will miss him as well for me, for he took something away

We spent many hours together on many a day

I feel now a hole where once he was

So along with the sorrow for him, he did what he often does

He retreats back to his cell, but this time for good

And lonelier now has become our neighborhood

I would have liked to say goodbye

To wish him well, and not to cry

I think of him lying now in the cold ground

Alone forever, I hope some peace he has finally found

Another friend has come and left

Is this the way of life – a form of theft?

Death or circumstance, no matter the reason

Life does indeed come with a dose of treason

My dog Edith. Darren loved to look into her eyes. I think he saw something there he could trust an love and who wouldn't hurt him.

A DISEASE CALLED E.A.S.E.

October 2018

A rhyme is perhaps an odd way to reflect on history. But the more I write, the more I let the words come by themselves. It's a throwback to a very old tradition practiced by those far more gifted in writing than myself – and for that I ask your indulgence. If you recall, I am a self-proclaimed "Seussian," as in Dr. Seuss, who raised important questions and provided a serious perspective in a whimsical format. I've often wondered if it was intentional, or if he saw his children or grandchildren facing some of life's dilemmas, and simply let his heart speak.

After many iterations, for I do try to review rationally (not for style, but for meaning) I have reached the limit of my skill as a poet.

To tell a story, one can't simply start in the middle, which is why I look backward, into the past, to see if I could identify a source, an explanation, a trend. I believe I did, and hopefully, it will resonate on some level with you. Mine is one perspective. There must certainly be others. It's not a question of who is right. That would be symptom of the problem and not an answer. But how to think about these things, being open minded yet wanting to put a stake in the ground from which, for reasons of personal experience, one feels most centered.

Poetry has a long and proud history, and I fear it has let itself slip out of its once principal position as the teller of important myths and tales, into the exaggeratedly personal. There is nothing wrong with this other than the subjective always runs the risk of losing the universal component of its message. Though we are all individuals, there is a common thread of humanity based on our physical and mental capacities, which we all share. Somewhere on our road to prosperity, we have lost this sense of unity or experience and of purpose..

That is just the point of this poem and its message. Once, for reasons inherent in the precarity of life in other times, we needed each other. And individual alone had little chance of survival. And so small units – generally family related – formed to offer a greater likelihood to live another day. Progress led to further developments until we have reached a point where, in fact, we don't really need each other every day. And it is at that point that the common thread which fostered cooperation began to shred, transforming itself from collaboration to competition, enshrined in our capitalist system.

I am not saying our system is wrong, for a system only acquires an identity through those who practice its precepts. We tend to love to assign fault to impersonal, inanimate things – cowards that we be – to absolve ourselves of any culpability. Convenient in the short term. Costly in so many ways in the longer term. Ater all, what is a system but a collection of ideas created by those who, when no longer finding it useful, deny it more easily that they invented it. These impersonal forces, they are avatars, surrogates that can contain blame, but are defenseless, and can offer no meaningful reply..

My point? A place to begin thinking about how we got here, where we are going, if we have let the system direct us rather than ourselves refining the system to better serve an ever growing awareness of the interdependence of life. I think that's what progress actually means – always looking forward to the better and not backward to what was, by definition less. If someone tries to convince you that the good old days were that good, then why did we try so hard to leave them behind? Are we not forgetting all the convenience, comfort, security and pleasure that is so readily available, along with the absence of hunger, pestilence, poverty and ignorance.

We fail to realize that over time, we have moved the baseline, as if today is the starting point, the guarantee that what is cannot be damaged or lost. Nothing could be more fallacious. What we have we can keep only if we care for it and everything, and everything, that supports it. Though we may choose not to "over-analyze" these interdependencies, what are we really doing if not going backwards to a time when things were not at all – at least materially – a bountiful as they are today.

What could we lose? Our institutions which guarantee our freedom and security. Our level of economic success and the comfort it brings. Our cultural achievements and the pleasure and meaning they bring. And perhaps most frightening of all, this marvelous Creation, with all its creatures and bounty, might be close to being damaged to a point where we will no longer have a home here. Oh, one more thing. We could very well lose ourselves.

Comfort. Wealth. Ease. These are all toxic when pushed to excess. We become inebriated with our own self importance by losing touch with the real sense of how we fit into a much larger whole. To lose one's humility is to lose one's soul. And without our soul, what are we really?

There is a plague sweeping the nation

Tearing us apart, a national disintegration

Talk abounds as we drown in noise

While scrupulously we avoid the source as it destroys

It started over 100 years ago

Does that surprise you, and how do I know?

Something called a good education

Not one focused mostly on socialization

To study history, learn something of the past

Trends exist and a long shadow they cast

Our intellectual traditions have changed over time

The emphasis evolves slowly; doesn't turn on a dime

From Greece to Rome, from Rome to the Popes

Dark Ages were a time when most were ignorant, if not dopes

But somehow we emerged from superstition and fear

The Renaissance brought a new kind of spirit more near

The Nation State emerged, people unified

No longer split into warring pieces when so many died

The Romantic period gave birth to love and art

Until the Age of Reason set to break it apart

The Mind not the Heart took precedence

A new future emerged from the present tense

Empires were built, ideas took form

Industry and the cities became the new norm

Where power and a wealth of a kind rarely seen

Fueled an explosion, often greedy and mean

There were wars to mark the death of an age

Kings destroyed themselves in a foolish rage

And with the old order, no longer there

There was a desire to build a world more fair

Gone were those who dictated rules and laws

Their strict hold on our values revealed its flaws

A new age began whose purpose was clear

It was time to deconstruct what was built on tradition and fear

First artists from the early nineteen hundreds broke with
convention

Out with the inheritance; time for new invention

Freud revealed to the world we were more than what we knew

Questions, if ever asked, were looked at askew

Wars of the World came to finish the task

It was time to rebuild, not a time to ask

What we knew was that our own answers we must find

On what values to build, the best for our time and our kind?

Communism came, now replaced by *gangsterism*

Convention was subjected to all forms of derision

It was now the age of me, casual the new rule

Whoever sees value in formality must be simple or a fool

Why do what I'm told, now I should do as I please?

I've got enough money and can live at my ease

I don't need my neighbor, we now compete

Why help another when what I want is their defeat?

For in this age of me, when only I count

The rules that impede my progress, in any amount

Deprive me of what is my God given right

To know no limit to my greed, and be ready to fight

For if the government comes to take what is mine

What I claim to have built all alone, and that's fine

I'll take out my guns and shoot any who dare

Who will challenge my kingdom of the ground and the air

But here's the hitch, there's one point forgotten

No one does it all alone, with myself besotten

It's you, my friend, whose world has shrunk

With money your only measure, you ignorant drunk

We built a new world after the Second World War

Prosperity and peace for all was to be the new door

We would walk through together, as together we rebuilt

Noble in victory we were, no need for guilt

The millions who died to pay for the peace

Maybe they are responsible for our ultimate release

But without rules or structure, when things come with great ease

We forget our purpose and think only ourselves to please

Our kind needs a challenge, a target, a goal

Without it we revert to greedy robbers who stole

Who forget we were not here first, others lived here before

Do you remember what happened to them when we came onshore?

Be they beast or human, nothing stood in our way

We degraded them all, and continue to this day

A vile species are we, selfish and mean

With short moments of goodness spaced in between

We make ourselves blind to what we do

We dig our own holes as if we barely knew

Forgetting that actions have consequences, a price to pay

And the bill always comes due, maybe even today

Remember JFK and his call to the nation?

Not to do something because it's easy, therein lies no salvation

But to do something hard, one that challenges creation

And prove to ourselves we have the required dedication

To something bigger, more important than us

When called up to serve, neither cry nor fuss

Instead we have we have grown lazy of mind?

Any problem we meet, rather than the true cause to find

To look beyond the symptom and discover the source

But that would require time, courage and conviction, of course

We'd rather call a doctor, take pills, anything but think

A band-aid on a cancer, how can this ship not sink?

Superficial, lazy, indulged and ignorant by choice

Those who praise the president, who listen to his voice

We say it is him for this havoc he unleashed, bearing his name

Is he he alone who should bear the blame?

Sixty million voted for, half the nation too tame

I say it is those who support him still who must now bear the
shame

Of their ignorance, it is something we choose or avoid

To look first to ourselves when our comfort is destroyed

Did we do all we could or did we close our eyes?

Did we give in to our anger and embrace the lies?

Did we have more children than we could support?

Birth control and adoption exist, so why abort?

This argument over right to life or to choose

Is a false one where no one wins and even the unborn lose

Think first, be sure of your acts

Don't come crying for help after the facts

That being said it is always a matter of choice

No one should impose their will or seek to drown out a voice

Like slavery, is this question worth destroying our nation

What would be gained if unwanted children were denied salvation?

Ignorance is no excuse for avoidable mistakes

Making everything a medical issue won't put on the brakes

Healthcare costs rise inexorably

Are we talking about the right things? Maybe?

Anxiety, drugs, opioid addiction

Among the young, is it fact or fiction?

Or is it part of the disease where guides have abandoned their task

Children need answers, not parents who questions ask

Like children ourselves we clamor for leaders to fulfill every need

Come restore us to our previous inglorious state of greed

If 60 million Americans voted for the Trump

The rest of us must accept that in the road this is no bump

He may have brought them together, but they were there in
wait

Angry at anyone but themselves, in need of someone to blame
and hate

Can the kind of ignorance which comes with ease

Be fought with a pill like any other disease?

Or is the cure one of the mind?

When the fever breaks and the search begins for answer to
find

Succeed we did, and live in the search of ever more ease

Children, raised with no knowledge that this is a disease

For neither want not hunger did they ever know

Look how tall and healthy they did grow

What did we teach them but the world awaits?

Great they are and will be, ready to run through the gates

To seize the golden apple, the oyster waits there

To win is all. Only losers think of fair

Self-esteem they may have in copious amounts

But real confidence and perspective, that's what counts

Never did they have a chance to discover their true worth

Their parents solved every problem, leaving them in dearth

Of challenges to take the true measure of themselves

They might as well have been born magical elves

Out into the world they go, perfect, or so they were told

Arrogant is not the same thing as bold

Failure was waiting to play its part

But this time something was missing on their life's chart

When difficulty came, so sure of success

Lost and confused when they fell into a mess

"Everyone told me how smart I would be

How is it so many fail to see?

Who wants to work in an office, I need to be free

After all, I was raised but to be me."

Good luck with that, so far as I know

The demand for me's in industry is not likely to grow

Become a filmmaker, write a novel, or knit

Or maybe take some time to work out and be fit

"Don't worry, for you are the image of me

A success you must at all costs be

I'll fix it up, make a few calls

Just be happy and don't worry about those falls"

"It wasn't your fault, how could that be?

Can we sue whomever, is the lawyer free?"

And so it goes, we've created a world deconstructed

No rules, no caring, no real education nor manners conducted

Have we arrived too soon at our destination?

Is this the end of the idea on which we founded this nation?

Will ease be the disease, the ultimate negation?

Will we like at the next iteration?

A people without a purpose have no reason to exist

Will the negative impulses we know grow stronger and persist?

Will they find their strength or from all effort desist?

Or will we wake up from the dream and know how to resist?

An exaggeration of the world of today

A caricature, an observation, perhaps just my way

To shock us out of the torpor, this ugly vision

It's really up to us to make that decision

We are powerless only if we choose to be

We have a system based on opportunity

Roadblocks exist, and they need to go

But waiting around for it to be so

Won't help us now, what future to seek out?

But if we show up and see once again what life is about

At times easy, often hard, there is no simple way

It's only by staying in the game for real can we have any say

Mitchell Ritter was born in New York City, a product of the public school system, he attended Colgate University where he graduated with degrees in History and Philosophy. Initially destined for a legal career, a series of serendipitous events led him to leave for Switzerland for degrees in Clinical and Developmental Psychology (L'Universite de Geneve etait le centre des etudes Piagetiennes). The focused being cognitive development in children, he undertook a training in Analytical Psychology at the C.G. Jung Institute. Though unintentional, this duality was to be the hallmark of his career.

After several years working in his chosen field, and while maintaining his private practice, he began a different career in the world of business. First in consulting, IT, Consumer Products, Pharmaceuticals across Europe and in the United States.

Returning back to his native New York in 2002, he began a journey or rediscovery which he has shared in his writings. His surprising choice of what he jokingly refers to as the "Seussian Style, " as in Dr. Seuss, reflects his very human view on himself and others. Returning to a classical time when stories were told in rhyme so as to be both heard, repeated and preserved, he also found that whereas prose tends to pursue a predetermined objective, poetry is more open ended, often producing new and unsuspected insights.

Prose, he says, is explicative, linear, logical. Poetry is evocative, metaphorical and emotional. Bringing the two together can be a challenge at first, for we are always in a hurry, wanting the bullet points, the top line, the short version. Life is much too complicated to comprehend if we approach it on the run. We need time to digest, assimilate, repurpose. Ignoring this produces superficial results, deprived of nuance, sentiment and true understanding.

Some friends have told him to be more concise. That would make perfect sense. But then, why not spend a bit more time in a world we have lost touch with, and which w desperately need to rediscover.

Time, he has said, is all we have. And we waste so much of it. But concision, compactness, the old quick and dirty are themselves a waste. Like a good meal, to be memorable and have a durable place in one's life, we need to savor each flavor, every texture, and the pleasure it procures. Wolf it down and you've missed the experience. These poems are what he likes to call a buffet of tappas. Not meant to be read as one would read a novel or biography, rather they are for tasting one at a time, depending on which one tempts you on a given day. You might not make the same selection on another day, and that is the point. The unconscious, something we seem to have forgotten because we can't stick electrodes in it or cut it up at an autopsy (nor does modern

science take much interest in it because their logical predisposition precludes any understanding on their part). But it's always there, a limitless space where anything and everything is possible. The laws of physics, biology or much else apply there. It's the seat of our imagination, our creativity, of many of the answers to problems we can't seem to crack if only we knew how to speak its language. And for these reasons, it represents a theme which, by no means "out there," the author reveals in the most practical of its expressions.

Father of two daughters, four granddaughters, and two dogs (owner, not father), he is an avid tennis player and an engaged conversational partner. His views, deeply inspired by the thinking of both Piaget and Jung, surprise some here, for they reflect the many perspectives which have found a unified home in his views. He lives, practices and writes in Carnegie Hill on the Upper East Side.

Yes, we are that complicated, and more.…

The Human Equation is a work in constant progress or regression. Nothing stands still. There is always a choice… Will we have the wisdom to make the right one?..

From the same author and available in either paperback or ebook formats on Amazon.com:

Mr. Hide's Progress – a short story about why people make the wrong choices

Six Years: - an expatriate's return to his native New York and how both he and how we can't always come home

In the Severth Year – the follow-on to Six Years and the effects of "reverse" culture shock

The Leftovers of God's Anger – a true story about what can happen to children who never knew what it meant to be loved, yet tried until they couldn't any more

The Prophet – Dead ends and other perils await those who choose to look away instead of ahead

Dawn or Dusk? – We are at a turning point in our nation's history. How we have changed, why, and it is always a choice

The Problem with Problems – We are at a turning point in our nation's history. We have strayed from who we always we thought we were and entered a no man's land where our war on formality, structure and convention has left us with little of sufficient solidity to build on. There remains always a choice. The question is do we still believe it?